THE JOB SEARCH MANUAL

THE
JOB SEARCH
MANUAL

Linda Aspey

ll.
2000

Copyright © Linda Aspey 1995

All rights reserved. No part of this publication may be reproduced, stored in a retrieval system, or transmitted in any form or by any means, electronic, mechanical, photocopying, recording, or otherwise without the prior permission of the publishers.

First published in Great Britain in 1995 by Management Books 2000 Ltd
125a The Broadway, Didcot, Oxfordshire OX11 8AW
Tel: 01235-815544. Fax: 01235-817188

Printed and bound in Great Britain by
WBC Book Manufacturers, Bridgend

This book is sold subject to the condition that it shall not, by way of trade or otherwise, be lent, resold, hired out, or otherwise circulated without the publisher's prior consent in any form of binding or cover other than that in which it is published and without a similar condition including this condition being imposed upon the subsequent purchaser.

British Library Cataloguing in Publication Data is available

ISBN 1-85252-255-0

Grateful thanks to: Marcus Carlton of White Morgan & Co., Independent Financial Advisers, for his invaluable help with the section on Financial Planning; and Ian Eaglestone, FIPD, for his helpful suggestions and comments and for patiently proofreading the manuscript.

Also my thanks to the many job seekers I have worked with over the past few years, without whom this book would not have been written: their experiences, trials and tribulations have been a unique learning experience for me.

FOREWORD

The 1990s have caused us all to stand back and assess the skills we need to survive in this world of work. We have seen right-sizing, business re-engineering, new technology and skills shift overlaid with recession. We are left facing new challenges and wondering about the future shape of our lives and careers.

Whichever euphemism we use, the result of these changes has meant unemployment has touched most of us. Managers have had to learn how to tell long-standing friends and colleagues they no longer have a job. Individuals have found themselves ill-equipped for job search in a small, highly competitive pool. Human resources professionals have limited tools – and time – as budgets dry up and outplacement is limited to a few senior staff.

What do we do for people who have been with an organisation for some years and only remember vaguely job hunting: people whose position and status have grown from experience rather than from learning and whose jobs are unique to one organisation?

This book provides an invaluable tool for both the HR professional and the job hunter. It contains useful, practical advice of assessing personal strengths and planning and executing an effective and successful job search. It helps the job hunter to approach the otherwise daunting task of looking for employment with hope and confidence.

We now have a well-written handbook which offers something for everyone involved in job search from an author who has both the intellectual and practical skills to help those people who get help from an outplacement programme.

Kathy Griffiths, MIPD, Head of Personnel,
The Financial Times Group

CONTENTS

Foreword vii

Introduction 1

1. The Marketing Campaign – Assessing What You Have 6

2. The Marketing Campaign – How Do I Action My Job Search? 18

3. Financial Planning – What Is My Budget? 21

4. Product Presentation – Your CV 32

5. The Target Market – Who Will Buy Me? 58

6. Product Presentation – Covering Letters, Applications Forms
   and Telephone Applications 90

7. Interviews 106

8. The Negotiation and Sale – The Offer and Starting Your New Job 125

Index 129

INTRODUCTION

This manual is written for people of all ages who, for whatever reason, are seeking a career move. The aim is to give you a practical, step-by-step guide to embarking on and completing a successful and professional job search campaign. There are lots of ways to find a fulfilling career: this manual is primarily concerned with job seeking, hence for retraining, self-employment, or specific types of occupation, I have included suggestions for further research and reading.

In or out of a recession, there are jobs available; the news headlines only tell us about the numbers of job losses – 'one in ten unemployed during 1994'. But what about the nine in ten who were working, moving jobs, successfully retraining, changing career entirely, setting up in their own business, etc.? Good news rarely makes the headlines.

You simply have to work much harder at finding a job nowadays – offers will not come plopping automatically onto the doormat, you have to go out and make them happen. Our methods of job seeking are tried and trusted, and this manual will give you the tools you need to maximise your chances – the hard work, commitment and persistence must come from you.

Unemployment – Disaster or Opportunity?

Unemployment, whatever the cause, can be a demoralising time both for you and for those close to you. It's difficult not to feel negative; it disrupts your family and social life, your financial security, your career progression and, most of all, knocks your confidence.

All in all it can feel like a disaster. But many people have found that it has been a time of opportunity – a time to reflect, re-evaluate and make changes. It does force you to look more closely at your life, for when you are busy working you simply do not have the time to stop and think 'Is this really want I want to do?'

The first phase of unemployment, and particularly redundancy, is often one of disbelief, followed by anger, guilt and then gradual acceptance. Others may actually be relieved, having felt trapped in the wrong job or knowing that something was going to happen sooner or later – i.e. 'the writing was on the wall'. Everyone's situation will be different. For some people, this may be a positive time, for others, quite the opposite. Hence this manual does not say 'Never mind, it will all be OK, you'll find something soon'. It will be tough, but whatever your feelings about being unemployed, there are some things which you can do to help you through this phase.

Getting yourself active and in a positive frame of mind as soon as possible is important – but there is little value in running around like a headless chicken! I suggest that you take some time out for a day or so to read this manual before you get your campaign started.

Looking at Things in Perspective

The word 'unemployed' has lost a lot of its stigma

We all know someone who is unemployed or who has been – most people are far less suspicious about your being unemployed than they would have been a few years ago.

Go for gold but be prepared to make realistic compromises

Do go for what you want, but be realistic and flexible. You might need to take a different job, at a lower status, in a different area, at lower pay, or you might have to take a course or a part-time job until the market picks up. Have a standby plan to fall back on and try to think of this as an opportunity to develop a new skill, or as a stepping stone.

Do not cut yourself off from people

Family and friends can help you in your job search, through their support, their ideas and their contacts. Although money will be tight, do keep in touch with people – they will help you more than you think. Keeping a balance between your job search and social life also helps to keep your spirits up and puts your situation into perspective.

Look after yourself

When you have done a good day's work at your job search, reward yourself with some physical activity or at least make sure you get some fresh air. Your physical state has a direct effect on your mental state so do try to keep active.

Try to keep to a daily routine

It is very easy to lapse into getting up late, hanging around in your dressing gown until midday, and then making a half-hearted attempt to make a few calls or job applications. Job seeking is a full-time job in itself and a set routine will help you to adjust to being away from work or study (if you have just finished your education). It will also help your family to come to terms more easily with your situation, and if they see that you are busy you won't get diverted from your job search by being asked to do the decorating or baby-sitting!

The less there is to do, the less you feel like doing. By setting a daily routine you can avoid this, and even when you feel that you have exhausted all avenues, there are always other companies you can try (there are thousands of companies in the UK; just look at how many there are in your local Thomson's Directory for example).

Don't dwell on other people's prejudices

These do of course exist, but whatever your age, experience, shape, size, skin colour, accent, education and social class, etc., you cannot change people's opinions overnight. But you should remember that not everyone has these blinkered opinions. If you can make improvements to develop yourself, fine, go ahead, but a 55-year-old cannot become a 30-year-old to please an employer and neither can a 17-year-old convert six months' work experience into 20 years' worth.

If you feel that there are these sort of 'negatives' about you, do not make apologies for them; this makes them important to others, and they are probably not relevant to your abilities and qualities! You are a unique person, in your own right, with your own personality and skills and there are no 'norms' into which you can or should be forced.

Redundancy: your job was made redundant – not you

Redundancy is expensive in many ways to the employer – the disruption to the company and the retained staff, the financial settlements and the legal implications are a high price to pay for simply sacking someone. Staff cutbacks are normally a commercial decision, rarely taken lightly, and often as a last resort in order to keep the company going.

Often people feel victimised and ask 'why me?' Rumours that some redundancies are made because of personality clashes or poor performance are rarely true. (If it is true in your case, perhaps this is the time to look at what went wrong and see if there is anything you can learn from the experience.)

You may feel that you have been poorly rewarded for being a good and loyal employee. But if you are a naturally loyal person who puts a lot into the job, can you honestly say that you would have been happy giving anything else but your best at the time?

You cannot gain anything from having negative feelings about your ex-employer; being negative, bitter and depressed will mean that you are the one who will lose out the most – it will prevent you from carrying on a successful job search and your emotional state will be noticed by potential employers. The only way you can survive is by being positive and optimistic – if you have negative feelings, talk them through with a close friend, family member or counsellor to get them off your chest. The past is gone, it cannot be changed, but your future is your hands – look forward to it for your own sake – no one else's.

Taking legal action against your employer: to sue or not to sue?

Many people want to take legal action if they feel that they were unfairly selected for redundancy, either as a way of 'making the company pay' or to prove to other people that 'I am right and they were wrong'.

If you genuinely feel that the company acted wrongly, and that you owe it to yourself to take action, do bear in mind that the whole process can take a long time, during which your energies and emotions will probably be spent dwelling on the past and will be directed away from your job search. For the sake of a few hundred pounds' compensation you could lose out on your future.

If you are considering making a claim, are other employers in the market (especially in a specialised industry where everyone knows everyone) going to be put off from employing you when they hear you are suing? Or will a claim against your previous employer affect your references? Suing can also be costly, financially and emotionally, if you lose. Do weigh up all the pros and cons carefully – talk it through with a friend or member of your family or friendly solicitor before you take formal legal steps. You and your future are the number one priorities now, and any decisions you make whilst under emotional stress may not be ones that you would make under less traumatic circumstances.

1. THE MARKETING CAMPAIGN

Assessing What You Have

Before you actually get down to doing anything about looking for jobs, you need to take stock of yourself and your life. It is far better to stop and think about your next career move rather than frantically running around in all directions without knowing where you are heading.

Taking stock means looking at what you have in life and what you want next. This includes your skills, abilities, strengths, weaknesses, experience, qualifications, how you work, what your goals are, what motivates you, where other people fit into the picture, and so forth – in other words, knowing and assessing yourself, and having a clear picture of what you have already achieved and what you want to achieve next.

It may help you to consider yourself as the marketing manager of a product – the product is you. You need to really know everything about yourself to see your potential and capabilities, so that you can turn these qualities into positive selling points in your job search, much like a marketing manager would do when launching a product. In addition, there are the very personal elements of knowing what you want and how that fits into the rest of your life, much like the marketing manager has a goal or aim for the product.

Knowing and assessing yourself is never easy, especially when it comes to seeing what you are good at. It is much easier to say 'I'm not much good at that' than it is to say 'I'm really good at that'. We rarely enjoy boasting or blowing our own trumpet, perhaps we feel it is simply 'not done'. But if you do not, who will? This manual will show you how to launch a unique product onto the market – you!

The Marketing Campaign – Assessing What You Have

The marketing manager needs to consider:
(not actually in this order but the principles are the same)

You need to think about:

The marketing campaign aims	What do I want?
Product	What am I selling?
Product strengths	Why would they want to buy me? How would I benefit them?
Product weaknesses	What might deter them from buying?
Marketing action	How do I action my job search? How can I review my progress?
Financial planning	What is my living budget? What salary can I ask for?
The target market	Who will buy me? How and where will I find these buyers
Product presentation	How can I present myself well?

Here are some questions which can get you started. Keep your answers to this exercise, so that later on in your search, if you find that you are doing a 'headless chicken' act, you can remind yourself of what you really want, what skills you have to offer and where you are heading. Use extra paper if you need to, but keep it in a safe place.

MARKETING CAMPAIGN AIMS
What Do I Want?

- Would I move house for my job? If yes, where would I move to? If no, how far am I prepared to travel to get to work?

  ....
  ....
  ....
  ....

- Do I want to stay in the same line of work?

  ....
  ....
  ....
  ....

- If not, what would my three most ideal jobs be?

✍ (a) ....
....

✍ (b) ....
....

✍ (c) ....
....

- Does this seem realistic? Do I have the skills and experience necessary?

✍ ....
....
....
....

- If not, how do I develop them? What would stop me from doing this?

✍ ....
....
....
....

- Do I like to be left to get on with a job or do I prefer to have guidance and support?

✍ ....
....
....
....

- Do I find I lose interest quickly in the job in hand and want to start something new? If yes, does this mean I need more variety? If no, does this mean I like to work mostly on one thing at a time?

✍ ....
....
....
....

- Am I prepared to retrain or upgrade my skills? If so, what am I interested in?

  ✎ ....

  ....

  ....

  ....

- If this meant studying, working long hours or having less money, can I really do it?

  ✎ ....

  ....

  ....

  ....

- What responsibilities do I enjoy taking on?

  ✎ ....

  ....

  ....

  ....

- What responsibilities would I prefer *not* to have?

  ✎ ....

  ....

  ....

  ....

- What did I like most about my last two jobs?

  ✎ ....

  ....

  ....

  ....

- What did I dislike most about my last two jobs?

  ✎ ....
  ....
  ....
  ....

- Do I prefer working in a large or small organisation?

  ✎ ....
  ....
  ....
  ....

- Why?

  ✎ ....
  ....
  ....
  ....

- Who else should I take into account when planning my future career?

  ✎ ....
  ....
  ....
  ....

THE PRODUCT – What Am I Selling?

- Which of the following words or phrases best apply to me? (Be honest with yourself here and tick all the relevant ones!)

☐ A doer	☐ Efficient	☐ Organised
☐ A loner	☐ Entertaining	☐ Passive
☐ A perfectionist	☐ Enthusiastic	☐ Patient
☐ A team player	☐ Experienced	☐ Persevering
☐ A thinker	☐ Excitable	☐ Practical
☐ Accurate	☐ Extroverted	☐ Proud
☐ Active	☐ Fast	☐ Quiet
☐ Adaptable	☐ Flexible	☐ Rebellious
☐ Argumentative	☐ Forgetful	☐ Relaxed
☐ Assertive	☐ Fun	☐ Reserved
☐ Aggressive	☐ Gentle	☐ Sensitive
☐ Bad-tempered	☐ Happy	☐ Serious
☐ Bubbly	☐ Having initiative	☐ Single-minded
☐ Bossy	☐ Helpful	☐ Slow
☐ Bored	☐ Humorous	☐ Snappy
☐ Busy	☐ Immature	☐ Stressed
☐ Capable	☐ Impatient	☐ Strong
☐ Caring	☐ Insecure	☐ Stubborn
☐ Cheeky	☐ Insensitive	☐ Supportive
☐ Committed	☐ Intelligent	☐ Thorough
☐ Communicative	☐ Interested	☐ Tidy
☐ Consistent	☐ Introverted	☐ Understanding
☐ Contented	☐ Irritable	☐ Unhappy
☐ Creative	☐ Keen	☐ Untidy
☐ Cruel	☐ Kind	☐ Valuable
☐ Decisive	☐ Lazy	☐ Versatile
☐ Dedicated	☐ Light-hearted	☐ Weak
☐ Disorganised	☐ Loyal	☐ Willing
☐ Disruptive	☐ Motivated	
☐ Effective	☐ Mature	

If this list makes you think about your 'faults' as well as your positive personal qualities, perhaps now is a good time to address them. If, for example, you were honest enough to describe yourself as lazy, it could be that you were in a job that didn't motivate you to do more. Or if you felt that you were irritable, it could be that there was something causing you a lot of stress. These are things to think about when you look at what you want from your next job.

- How else would I describe myself? How would my closest friend and workmates describe me?

✎ ....
....
....
....

- Have I had any training at work and what did I learn from it?

✎ ....
....
....
....

PRODUCT STRENGTHS – Why Would They Want To Buy Me?

- What do I generally do best at work? What is it that makes me enjoy it?

✎ ....
....
....
....

- What did I do for my last two employers that made me feel I was really useful to the company?

✎ ....
....
....
....

The Marketing Campaign – Assessing What You Have

- Why did these employers take me on (rather than anyone else) in the first place? (Try to think of at least three reasons.)

✍ (a)...

✍ (b)...

✍ (c)...

- What would I see as my three main achievements?

✍ (a)...

✍ (b)...

✍ (c)...

- Have I been praised for something at work?

✍ ....
....
....

- What would I see as my three main strengths?

✍ (a)...

✍ (b)...

✍ (c)...

PRODUCT WEAKNESSES –
What Might Deter Them From Buying?

- Do I see my age as being a problem? If yes, what skills, personal qualities or experience do I have to overcome this?

  ✍ ....
  ....
  ....
  ....

- What do I generally do *worst* at work? Why is that?

  ✍ ....
  ....
  ....
  ....

- Are there any skills that I feel I lack? If so, what I can do about this?

  ✍ ....
  ....
  ....
  ....

- What would I see as my three main weaknesses?

  ✍ (a) ....
  ....
  ✍ (b) ....
  ....
  ✍ (c) ....
  ....

- What could I do to tackle these weaknesses?

  ✍ ....
  ....
  ....
  ....

- Have I been criticised for something at work? If yes, what was criticised and did I learn anything from that?

✍ ....
....
....
....

Now make a list of what you see as your 'plus and minus points' using the table below. Put what you see as your 'positive' points on the plus side, and 'negative' points on the minus side.

The way you view the minuses will come across to other people, so try to find a plus point to match every minus. For example, if you don't like working with other people all the time the plus can be that you work well unsupervised and get on with things. If a minus is that you have not used a computer, the plus could be that you are going to start evening classes. When it comes to 'negative' personal characteristics, such as 'bossy', this could mean that you have leadership qualities (that perhaps just need to be adapted to become good supervisory skills).

PLUSES	MINUSES

You will hopefully have begun to see a clearer picture of you – the product. Now, you can start to put it all together, using your 'taking stock' questions and your 'pluses and minuses'.

MY THREE IDEAL (AND REALISTIC) JOBS

Position

✍ (a)...
....

✍ (b)...
....

✍ (c)...
....

Key responsibilities I would like

✍ (a)...
....

✍ (b)...
....

✍ (c)...
....

✍ (d)...
....

Key skills I have to offer

✍ (a)...
....

✍ (b)...
....

✍ (c)...
....

✍ (d)...
....

Type of company or organisation

✍ ....
....
....
....

Type of people/structure I would prefer

✍ ....
....
....
....

Location

✍ ....
....
....
....

Prospects

(a) One year from now I would like:

✍ ....
....
....

(b) Three years from now I would like:

✍ ....
....
....

For a more in-depth assessment of your skills and career and personal objectives, *Build Your Own Rainbow* is a useful book which I often recommend (published by Management Books 2000).

2. THE MARKETING CAMPAIGN

How Do I Action My Job Search?
How Can I Review My Progress?

Getting Organised

Just as you have everything in its proper place at work, you need to be as organised at home. For example, if at work a customer calls with a query you would need to know where their file is kept, what you last said to that person, and where you keep items such as stationery and stamps so that you can get suitable letters off promptly.

The same applies to your job search: imagine answering the telephone to someone calling about a job for which you have applied, and you have no idea of who they are, which job they are referring to, and there is no pen or paper by the telephone when you need it (there never is!). Or perhaps you see a job in the Sunday paper and want to get your application in the post for Monday morning, but have no stamps.

You can avoid these panic situations by organising your own temporary office. If possible, set aside a proper workspace where you have a desk or table, a telephone and all your job search tools at hand. Sitting on the sofa in front of the TV is not the best place to work – there are too many distractions for one thing and trying to write on your lap is never easy.

An answering machine is a real bonus so that you can go out without worrying about missing any important calls. If you do not have a telephone at home, invest in some phone cards – it is so much easier to talk without the pips interrupting you every three minutes.

If there is nowhere quiet at home, then for work that does not need a telephone you can use your local library (useful too for the photocopier).

Alternatively, do you know someone who runs their own business who would let you use their office space, perhaps in return for covering reception/telephone during lunch times?

Stationery Items and Record Keeping

You'll need quality writing paper and envelopes (the best you can afford), stamps and, if possible (although not essential), a typewriter or word processor. Large folders or box files are useful to keep copies of job adverts, photocopies of application forms sent out, letters sent and received from potential employers. You will need to keep track of who you have spoken or applied to, when, what the result was and so forth.

At the end of Chapter 5 are some forms (you can make copies) to keep records of all your job search activities. If you prefer, an index card system can be useful. A diary is essential – it is vital to ensure that you do not miss one appointment!

Your Action Plan

Most successful people plan their day by making a list of tasks to be completed and dealing with them in order of importance. As a result, their day runs more smoothly, nothing is neglected or forgotten and finishing these tasks gives them a feeling of accomplishment.

You also need to plan what you are going to do in your job search – to put it another way, would you go on holiday without deciding where you want to go, what you will be taking and how you are going to get there? An occasion such as a holiday is not an everyday event, and neither, until now, has been your job search. It is probably quite new to you so you will be much more successful if you do have a plan of action – it helps to monitor your efforts and to achieve what you set out to do.

So, like the marketing manager, you can plan your strategy, with timescales, marketing reviews and contingency plans – your own action plan. This plan should be realistic, achievable and reviewed at regular intervals to check your progress. Setting yourself tasks to do and deadline dates is particularly helpful: it is very easy to lose track of what is happening in your job search campaign when you have several activities going on at any one time.

Set Yourself Targets

It does help to set yourself a timetable and targets. What actual hours will you set aside to work: 9 am to 5 pm or every afternoon and early evening? How many jobs will you aim to apply for each week, how many new contacts by telephone and letter will you make per week? If you have targets written down you are much more likely to achieve them.

I suggest that you should aim to make at *least* thirty applications or contacts per week – that includes talking to people, applying to vacancies, seeing agencies and sending your CV to suitable companies. It sounds a lot, but it is only six a day in a working week.

Week one will be spent mainly on the stock-taking exercises, CV preparation and the more practical aspects of job loss – sorting out your finances and so forth. If you get yourself into a routine during this time, you will find it much easier to stick to it in the coming weeks.

Putting Your Action Plan Together

As you progress through this manual, you will learn more specific details about what you need to do to run a successful job search campaign. Chapter 5 gives an example of an action plan followed by a blank form which you can copy and use for your own weekly plan.

3. FINANCIAL PLANNING –

What Is My Budget?

You need to protect your interests and those of your family before you do anything else – domestic budgeting is even more important now. Whilst your financial situation may be good for a while, especially if you have received a lump-sum payment from your previous employer, you do need to think about the longer term and how you will cope in the unlikely event that you are on the job market for longer than anticipated.

Before you start your job search, go along to any interview or get into any discussions about salary, work out what you actually need – what are your monthly commitments? Make a list of these to get your absolute bottom line. Also think about what you will do if you can not get your bottom line: are there items which you can cut back on? Finances may be restricted at first, so it is a good idea to draw up a budget now with all your outgoings and incomings. At the end of this chapter is a budget planner which may be useful.

State Benefits

It is important to note that following the November 1993 budget, there were some major changes in benefits, particularly for the unemployed, which are being phased in during 1995 and 1996. The following information, therefore, is intended as only as a guideline to current state benefits, and is, as far as we are aware, correct as at June 1994.

Each claim is treated on its own merits by the Department of Social Security (DSS) and we are unable therefore to give specific advice (neither are we qualified to do so!). We strongly recommend that you check with the appropriate government agency in all cases. You may find it helpful in the first instance to contact the Social Security freeline service, which gives free telephone advice and general information on social security benefits. The telephone number is 0800-666 555.

There is a range of state benefits you may be entitled to if you become unemployed. It is worth investigating each one to establish if you can receive financial help until you find your next job. For current rates of benefits we advise you to check with your DSS.

First Steps

On the first day you are not working, contact (telephone or visit) your local Unemployment Benefit Office. Whether or not you are working your notice or are paid in lieu of notice, you must register as your National Insurance contributions will be paid for by the DSS.

You may not be entitled to any payments immediately, but you must find out for certain. Do not delay – claims cannot usually be backdated. The offices, listed under 'Government Offices' in Yellow Pages (subheadings: Employment Services and /or Social Security, Department of), are open 09.00-15.30, Monday to Friday. They will make an appointment for you to see a New Client Adviser (usually 3-5 days' time). If attendance at the nearest office would be difficult, ask whether any special arrangements can be made. Take your P45 and National Insurance number to the Benefit Office. If you do not have these, continue with your claim – you can send them in at a later date.

Benefit is paid every two weeks by Giro cheque, sent to you in the post after you have 'signed on'. You can cash it at the Post Office or pay it into your bank or building society account. When you register, you should tell them which account and branch you will use – you cannot just go to any branch.

The DSS publish a range of free leaflets on the various state benefits. They are also available from your local Post Office and include:

FB2 – Which Benefit? (a guide to all benefits)
IS20 – A Guide to Income Support
FB9 – Unemployed? (a general guide)
FB28 – Sick or Disabled?
NI 12 – Unemployment Benefit
RR1 – Housing Benefit
NI266 – How to Appeal

Financial Planning

Unemployment Benefit (UB)

Eligibility

UB is currently available to unemployed people who are capable of, available for, and actively seeking work (providing that you have no pensionable earnings in which case any entitlement to benefit will be affected). You will have to prove that you are seeking work when you make your first UB claim and thereafter to prove continuously you are available for and seeking work, so you must keep copies of job applications, letters, advertisements, interview letters, etc.

The amount of your savings or lump-sum severance pay makes no difference to UB (but if you have been paid in lieu of notice – for example, four weeks' pay – you are not officially unemployed until this paid notice period runs out). If you have taken voluntary redundancy you may not be entitled to UB – you must check with the DSS.

UB depends on your National Insurance (NI) contribution records. You must have paid Class 1 NI on wages earned of 25 times the lower earnings limit in the last tax year, and paid or have been credited with Class 1 contributions for 50 times the lower earnings limit over the last two tax years. (We said it was complicated!)

Credits for Class 1 NI are given for periods when you have been off work sick (and getting statutory sick pay or other invalidity or sickness benefit), or when you have been on UB before. If you have elected to pay NI at the reduced rate (i.e. 'reduced stamp') you will not be eligible for UB. If you are over 55, benefit could be reduced if your pension is more than a certain amount.

In all cases, the UB office will ask you to fill in the following forms:

UB461 – Claim Form
UB671 – Questionnaire concerning your availability for work

The benefit

You may get an extra payment if have an adult dependant or if you have someone looking after your children, but if your partner earns above a certain limit each week this may be reduced. Benefit is taxed as income.

UB is paid for one year, if you are continuously not working. After this time, if you are still not working, your claim will be reviewed and you may then become entitled to Income Support. You need to go to the UB office to 'sign on' every two weeks after your first claim, at the same time and day of the week.

Those on Unemployment Benefit may be able to claim travel expenses to and from interviews. You can ask at the UB office. If you make a claim the interviewer you met will usually be asked by the DSS if you did actually go to the interview.

In 1996 UB will be changed to 'Job Seeker's Allowance' and the rules will change, as will the length of time this benefit can be claimed.

Income Support (IS)

Whether or not you get UB, you may be entitled to Income Support. This is a means-tested benefit which aims to bring people on very low incomes up to a basic weekly rate. Because this benefit is means-tested, eligibility varies greatly from individual to individual. The rules on this will also change over the next two years.

Until the changes take place, you need to get an IS claim form (B1 Income Support), which you will be given when you register for UB (if you ask for one), and they will direct you to the local DSS. You may not get form B1 until UB671 is completed (see above).

Although eligibility does vary greatly, you need to be aware of two factors that will usually make you ineligible for IS:

- If your partner or spouse works 16 or more hours per week (regardless of how much they earn);

- If your household savings amount to more than £8,000. If your savings (or lump sum redundancy or payment in lieu of notice) amount to more than £3,000 at the time of claiming, the amount of benefit you receive will be reduced in proportion. Your local DSS office will tell you by how much.

If you do qualify for IS, you are entitled to 100 per cent Housing Benefit and help with your Council Tax (see below). If your application is refused, you can appeal against the decision.

Those with a mortgage who qualify for IS will receive help with their monthly mortgage payments: 50 per cent of your mortgage interest repayments are met by IS for the first 16 weeks on benefit, thereafter it will pay all the interest repayments (not the outstanding capital sum).

If you qualify for IS you may also get free: NHS prescriptions; dental treatment; eyesight tests; travelling to hospitals; milk; school meals – see Leaflet AB11 (Help with NHS costs).

There is also a Social Fund which is designed to help you to buy the basics of life such as clothing, furniture, etc. If you have more than £500 in savings you will not qualify. Form B1 has the relevant questions for the Social Fund.

Housing Benefit (HB)

Once again, this benefit is means-tested and the rules are complicated, so we recommend that you speak to your local Housing Benefits Department in the first instance if you are considering making a claim.

HB can pay your rent, whether you are a council or private tenant, or a member of a housing association. Eligibility depends on your household savings being less than £16,000, rather than £8,000 for IS. If you are on IS, you qualify automatically for 100 per cent HB, which will pay your rent, plus some other services under certain circumstances, although it will not pay for things like insurance or your water bills.

HB can be paid whether or not you are in work, so it is worth investigating whatever your circumstances. Your local authority runs the Housing Benefit Scheme, so contact the town hall for details.

Council Tax Benefit (CTB)

CTB operates in the same way and on the same basis as Housing Benefit. Those on Income Support may get a 100 per cent rebate, as do those whose household income is below an individually calculated amount, known as the 'applicable amount'. Even those who have incomes above the 'applicable amount' may be entitled to benefit in certain circumstances, so contact the Council Tax department of your local authority or obtain leaflet CTB1 (Help With the Council Tax) from a Post Office.

Sickness and Invalidity Benefits

If you are unemployed and claiming benefit and become incapable of work because of illness or disability, you may be entitled to Sickness Benefit (but this depends on your pensionable earnings). Entitlement also depends on having paid National Insurance contributions in the 'relevant' tax years, although under certain circumstances those without a good NI record may also be entitled.

If you have been on Sickness Benefit for 28 weeks, you become entitled to Invalidity Benefit, which lasts as long as you are incapable of work right up to retirement age. You may get extra for an adult dependant (e.g. non-working spouse) and for each dependent child. From April 1995 this benefit will become 'Incapacity Benefit' and, again, the rules and eligibility will change.

National Insurance (NI)

If NI has been deducted from your final wage when you are paid up to a certain period, then the DSS will take over when this period expires. If you have been paid a lump sum which has not been taxed or NI'd by your employer, you must see the DSS who will 'credit' you for NI, whether or not you are claiming UB.

It is important to keep up your NI contributions so that your right to benefits and pension in the future is not affected. If you cease to claim benefit, make sure your contributions resume with your new employer and check that you have an adequate level. If your record shows a shortfall you will be advised by the DSS. You can make up contributions. The Central Office which holds all NI records is: DSS Long Benton, Benton Park Road, Long Benton, Newcastle upon Tyne, NE98 1YX (Tel. 0191-213 5000).

Income Tax

It is not possible to obtain an immediate tax refund when you cease work. Any tax taken off wages paid to you since the start of the tax year is kept to cover the tax which has been paid on the benefit you receive.

When you stop claiming benefit or at the end of the tax year, the Benefit Office will send you any refund which is due. You can always talk direct to your Inspector of Taxes (they are normally very helpful) at the tax office holding your record. Your tax office will be shown on one of your tax papers.

Sorting out Your Other Finances

Financial advice

You may require advice on how best to reorganise capital, investments, pensions or severance pay. Use an Independent Financial Adviser (IFA), one that is a member of FIMBRA. You should check with the company that they are. Your brother-in-law may be a representative with one of the best insurance companies but you need *independent* advice! There will be a queue of people waiting to sell you investment advice and policies but it is *your* money and *your* future.

Mortgage

Please see your bank or mortgage adviser at the building society as soon as possible. If you keep people informed of your situation, they will trust you far more than if you leave it until things get out of control. Ask them about ways of reducing/deferring interest or extending the term of the mortgage. Obviously, some of the mortgage may be paid by DSS if you qualify for Income Support.

Rent

The same applies – keep the landlord informed and he/she may be willing to reduce the rent or defer payment for a while. They may feel that it is better to have a tenant who intends to pay in the future than no tenant at all!

Your pension

Each person's circumstances will vary according to their age, their length of service, etc. Normally there are three options:

- Do nothing – the accrued pension up to the date of leaving is likely to be revalued each year and paid to you at retirement age.
- Transfer to a new employer's scheme – most schemes will accept a transfer.
- Transfer to a private arrangement with an insurance company via an IFA.

You can ask your previous company about your pension options and they will usually be able to get you a statement of the value of your fund. An Independent Financial Adviser will be able to do this for you and explain all the implications.

Insurances

Consider your family commitments – partner, children, other relatives. It is not usually a good idea to surrender policies (you may get back very little, particularly if the policy is less than two years old). Consult your insurance adviser – they may be able to arrange a loan against the policy, often at rates far lower than a bank. If you have a young family, it is vital to keep up insurances. If your company paid your life insurance you might want to take out a low-cost life policy of some kind – again, you should see an IFA.

Debts

Help and advice

The Citizens' Advice Bureau can help with social security claims or negotiations on any debts. They are the most experienced body and, in the case of creditors, can often get a more positive reponse than you can as an individual. They will write letters on your behalf and also provide you with free legal advice. Their number is in Yellow Pages, under 'Social Service and Welfare Organisations'.

There are some initial steps that you can take to prevent debt problems escalating.

Credit cards

Talk to the company concerned: they may defer interest payments for a period. Their interest rates are so high that it may again be worth talking to your bank to see if they will lend you the money to pay off credit card debts. You could be sued or made bankrupt if the company chose to go that far should you make no effort to repay at least some of the debt.

Secured loans

These include, for example, loans secured on your house or second mortgages. Lenders will try their best to help you to keep your home and repossession is a last-ditch attempt to recover their money.

Fuel

Both the gas and electricity companies are more than willing to negotiate reduced payments as long as you talk you them. Do not wait until it is too late and you are about to be cut off. Power can be cut off without reference to the Court if you do not respond to the demands.

Maintenance / child support

The Court has the power to vary a maintenance order. You must inform the Court of a change in your circumstances. You are legally liable to pay, so negotiation is essential.

Hire purchase

It is illegal to sell something that is still being paid off on hire purchase, but you could perhaps take out a bank loan instead (the interest rates are lower), pay off the HP and then sell the goods if you wish. Ask the HP firm for a written statement. Any agreement regulated by the Consumer Credit Act will provide for a rebate of interest and other charges in the event of early settlement.

Some HP companies charge a penalty for early redemption of a loan – in some cases up to three months' interest will be charged to you. Check your agreement and obtain written confirmation of any such charges before you decide to redeem the loan.

Alternatively, HP interest payments could be deferred. It is rarely in your interest to return the goods – you have paid towards their purchase so all your payments will be wasted. Goods can be repossessed by the HP firm if you do not keep up payments.

Bailiffs

It is very often possible to negotiate with bailiffs. They do not have the right to force entry; they may however, gain access where a door is left open or unlocked. The Citizens' Advice Bureau will help you if you have problems.

Moneylenders

Never go to a moneylender or loan shark. They charge high rates of interest and can be a problem if you do not keep up payments. If you have used one, advise the police of any difficulties.

Financial Planning

Budget Planner

Item - expenditure	Monthly cost £	Quarterly cost £	Annual cost £	Possible savings? £	Weekly or monthly income	£weekly	£monthly
Mortgage/rent					Take home wages/salary		
Council Tax					Part - time work		
Water rates					Partner's income		
Gas					Other adult's contribution		
Electricity					Interest on savings		
Other fuel					State benefits:		
Food/drink/housekeeping					1		
Buildings insurance					2		
Contents insurance					3		
Life assurance					4		
Pensions/savings/investments					5		
Telephone					Interest on redundancy money		
Car tax/ car insurance					Other income, e.g. pension		
Petrol/oil/car expenses							
Train/bus/tube fares							
Hire purchase							
Credit/store card repayments							
TV/video rental/TV licence							
Child minder/creche							
Clothing/shoes							
School uniforms							
School meals/fees							
Newspapers/magazines							
Subscriptions/clubs							
Socialising expenses							
Sports expenses							
Holidays							
Presents/Christmas expenses							
Pocket money							
Other expenses							
Total estimated expenditure £	£	£	£	£	TOTAL INCOME	£	£
					Subtract expenditure from income	£	£
					Difference - surplus or excess	£	£

THE PRICING
WHAT SALARY CAN I ASK FOR?

In this highly competitive market, many people are unsure as to what salary they should be looking for – some employers have not given increases for some time, and are able to pay less than they would in a time of skills shortage when they have to pay more to attract the right people.

The question of whether or not you can afford to earn less is a very personal one – and how far (if at all) you are prepared to compromise between getting a job and being taken advantage of. It is a good idea to have two figures in mind: your 'ideal' salary and your 'acceptable' salary.

What you earned in your last job is not really all that relevant – you may have been over- or underpaid. It is best to look at each specific career or job in its own light: what are the responsibilities and what is the job worth? Also, bear in mind that the base salary you are looking for can be sometimes augmented with benefits or bonuses.

You can find out about the market rates by speaking to several employment agencies: average out their figures and you should be able to arrive at an approximate market rate. You may also have friends in similar jobs. Where you know them well enough, they may give you an idea of what they earn. Also, if you are going for a different role, perhaps you could ask your friends what their company pays for that type of job. For more information on negotiating salaries, see Chapter 8.

4. PRODUCT PRESENTATION

Your CV

Your curriculum vitae is one of the most useful tools you have in your job search – therefore it is always worth spending time and effort to get it looking good. It is, in effect, your 'marketing brochure'.

CVs are used more often to eliminate than to select people. The first task of anyone reading a batch of CVs is to discard those which are poorly presented or do not seem to be suitable and then concentrate on the rest. Therefore you must not give them any reason to discard yours at a glance – first impressions count. Your CV should:

- Get the reader interested enough in you to want to meet you so that you will have the opportunity to sell yourself to them face to face. The first page of your CV should be like a newspaper headline – easy to read, quick to make the point and making the reader want to carry on reading. Marketeers use 'AIDA', a way of reminding themselves what their brochures or letters should do: you need to attract **A**ttention, create **I**nterest, get their **D**esire, and make them want to take **A**ction.

- Show that you can present yourself professionally and that you could be an asset to the company.

- Show that you can do the job or, if you don't have the *all* the right qualifications or experience, that you have the ability to learn those aspects.

In order to make your CV stand out from the crowd you'll need to do more than just give a list of responsibilities and duties. Although curriculum vitae literally means 'list of life', one containing just a list of duties is lifeless and may not reflect what skills you really have.

Using 'Bridge' Words and Phrases

Should you find yourself getting stuck on how to turn your list of duties into something more interesting, try using a word or phrase to explain, such as: 'which resulted in....', 'which was used by...', 'in order to...', 'so that......' and so forth. Putting a positive, active emphasis on the tasks transforms them into a 'brochure' of yourself. Look at a few sales brochures – you will soon see the difference between a list of what the product actually does and how it can really benefit the buyer.

For example, if one of your responsibilities was to 'Process sales orders', this does not really show what skills you used or why it was beneficial to the company. However, 'Processed sales orders efficiently which reduced delivery time to customers by two days' says so much more about your skills and is much more interesting to the reader – it also reflects your efficiency and your attitude to the company.

Drafting your CV

Your experience was gained over a period of time and it is unlikely that you will be able to write a really good CV at the first attempt. It will take you some time to be happy with it, but it will be worth it when you have an end product that accurately reflects your experience and qualities. Have a look at the different styles in this manual, and perhaps go the library and look at one of the many books on CVs. You could also ask a friend to help you with your CV: they may be able to point out skills or experience about which you had forgotten.

Measure your Achievements and Be Specific

When you are writing about achievements, always try to qualify this with numbers or percentages. If you say that you were the 'Top Salesperson in 1991' you may have sold only one box while other salespeople sold none, or you may have been the only salesperson! It is much better to give exact figures – for example, 'Top Salesperson in 1991 out of four, achieving 105 per cent of annual target', or 'Good word-processing skills' can become 'WP speed 60wpm on IBM PC using WordPerfect 5.1'. People prefer specific, tangible statements.

Every Day You Accomplished Something

It's very easy to forget just what we contribute to a job on a day-to-day basis – particularly after a long time in one job. We just get on with things without analysing what it is we do. Here are some ideas on how to look for accomplishments:

- What did you do that helped someone else to do their job better?
- What did you change, improve or save?
- What responsibilities were you given?
- How did you use your own initiative?
- What would have been neglected if you had not been there each day?

Try asking yourself these questions:

- *What did I do for my employers which really contributed something to their business?* You were not just employed because you needed a job; you made a contribution to the business. What were your major contributions at each company?

- *Was I **P**roductive, **E**ffective, and did I help them to make a **P**rofit? ('PEP!')* Even if you were not selling something then the fact that you were, for example, helpful and polite to customers on the telephone will have added to the company's reputation and therefore increased business.

- *What skills have I got to offer another company?* You had something to offer to your last company – what about the next one? What skills did you use that will benefit someone else, and how can you highlight these?

Try these positive words and phrases – you can use them to show what you are, do or did:

A doer	Assisted	Designed
Ability/able to	Built	Doubled
Accomplished	Capable of	Eliminated
Accurate	Completed	Efficient
Accustomed	Contributed	Effective
Achieved	Created	Enhanced
Acted as	Decided	Established
Adaptable	Developed	Expanded
Arranged	Demonstrated	Enjoyed

Product Presentation – Your CV

Experienced	Organised	Set up
Flexible	Ordered	Skilled
Generated	Performed	Started
Helped	Planned	Successfully
Implemented	Processed	Supervised
Improved	Produced	Trained
Increased	Profitable	Thorough
Initiated	Processed	Upgraded
Introduced	Promoted	Utilised
Keen to	Reduced	Valuable
Launched	Reorganised	Versatile
Maintained	Repaired	Willing
Monitored	Revised	Won
Motivated	Saved	Worked with
Negotiated	Scheduled	
Operated	Serviced	

Your CV style

Everyone has a different style of presenting a CV and every recruiter has their own opinion about what they like. It is best, therefore, to stick to a neat, short and positive CV that is not long winded or 'flashy'.

One or more CVs?

You may want to have several CVs for different jobs, but unless you keep track of which one you sent to which company, you may get a little confused. A general one which draws attention to your key skills and experience is best; your covering letter can be tailored to specifically match the job or company.

Golden Rules:

- Use good-quality plain unlined white or cream A4 paper. Your CV must be typed or word-processed – never hand-written (unless you are asked for one). Do not use glossy covers or photographs (unless a photograph is requested) – recruiters usually dislike them.

- Keep to a maximum of three pages, ideally two. Avoid overcrowding and irrelevant detail; it should be easy to read quickly – you only have a few seconds to make an impact!

- Your CV should say more about your most recent experience – for example, your last three jobs or positions – with a brief description of your earlier work and employers.

- *Always* be positive and sell your strengths. Ask yourself 'What have I got to sell?' Remember PEP and bring in relevant proof whenever you can.

- Be accurate with dates (include months as well as years) and if there are any gaps in your work history, give a brief, positive explanation.

- Keep it neat, grammatically correct, and check your spelling – get someone else to read the final version. If you can afford to have it typed professionally, it will be a worthwhile investment, and you can keep the original copy in clean condition so that you can photocopy spares.

- Never lie about non-existent qualifications or work experience. If you do you will probably get found out, or you may have difficulty at an interview when you are put on the spot.

- Avoid using jargon. The person first reading your CV may not be a specialist in your field and may not understand, and you could lose out.

Ask Someone's Opinion

When you have written your CV, if you have a business contact whose opinion you value, ask them to read it through as if they were recruiting someone. If there are any gaps in information, questions left unanswered, or the CV does not do you justice, an outside viewpoint can often help.

Remember What You've Written

Make sure that you memorise your CV. If you cannot remember what you did and when, it does create a poor impression at interview. Carry your CV with you at all times: you never know who you may meet or bump into – they may be able to help you.

Product Presentation – Your CV

Overview of CV content

(All the points marked * can be put on the last page of the CV if you prefer.)

Name	Your full name.
Address	Your full address, including postcode.
Telephone no.	Your home and/or work number if you can take calls at work.
Date of birth	* If you feel that your age ('too young or too old!') is likely to go against you, your personal details can be put on the last page at the end of the CV
Nationality	* As above – although discrimination is illegal, there are still some offenders out there. It's up to you to decide how you feel about this.
Marital status	* You do not have to give this if you do not wish to – although it still is the 'norm'.
Education	* From secondary school upwards. Include the years, name of the school, examination subjects and grades. If it is more than about ten years ago 'O' level grades are not necessary (unless they were all A grades!). It is not essential to put your education on the first page if you have good work experience (or no formal educational qualifications).
Further Education	* Details of colleges of further education. Some people may want to separate 'Further' (college) and 'Higher' (university/polytechnic education) but this is not essential. Give name of establishment, dates, subjects studied and grades obtained. Include evening classes.
Training/Skills	* Details of any special skills such as speaking a foreign language, computing or word-processing skills and systems used, HGV licence, etc. Include any awards or extra training and any professional qualifications.

If the training is very relevant to your career, *keep it on page one.*

Resumé This is optional but can be used to give the reader a brief 'snapshot' description of what you are and what your achievements are.

CAREER HISTORY

From (month & year) Present or most recent employer – company name and location (full address is not necessary). You can put a brief explanation of the industry your company is in, its products and services, and its size, to create another 'snapshot'.
To:

Position If you have had several roles or been promoted within the company, list them and put the dates next to them in brackets.

Salary If you are highly paid, overpaid or underpaid then your salary could put them off. On the other hand, if you know you want the same salary, it will give the reader an idea of your 'level'. If in doubt, leave it out.

Responsibilities Describe, don't just state your responsibilities. (Try using some of the words from pagew 34-5). Bullet points (like this •) are useful in drawing attention to your responsibilities and help to break up the text.

Reason for leaving If you wish to include this (it is optional), keep it positive even in a negative situation. If you left due to redundancy, keep it brief – e.g. 'Company restructured resulting in several redundancies'. Do not make it personal.

Previous employers Continue in the same way, listing previous employers in reverse chronological order (i.e. most recent first). Remember that previous employment details should be briefer than recent ones.

Interests DIY or gardening are things that most people do, so only put your interests in if they are likely to be interesting. Never include what could be seen as contentious such as dangerous sports or strongly political activities. Keep this side of personal life personal!

Referees — Not usually necessary as part of your CV (unless you are a student) and unlikely to sway the reader towards seeing you. If you do wish to include them, always check with your referee first and find out what type of reference they are likely to give. If it is not glowing then ask another person who will give you a good reference!

Sample CVs

Page 1	CURRICULUM VITAE

Name	JOHN B COLES
Address	10 Walker's Way, Petts Wood, Kent. TN12 2TZ
Telephone	01980-246810
Date of birth	4.10.1968 Marital status: Married
Nationality	British

Education

1990 to date	East Kent College
	ACCA Stage 1 and two papers Stage 2 completed (half day release and evening class)
1979 – 1984	Petts Wood Comprehensive, Kent
	6 CSEs: Accounts (B); Maths (C); Economics (C); English (C); Biology (C); History (D)

Resumé

I am a hard-working and adaptable individual, with good experience of maintaining accounts for small, growing and large businesses. I enjoy both working alone or within a team, and I am keen to use my own initiative. I have commenced professional studies and am committed to qualifying within the next two years. Areas of experience include banking, reconciliations, purchase and sales ledger, all aspects of PAYE, Schedule D, VAT and computerised accounting.

Employment History

September 1987	Peter's Brasserie Ltd, Petts Wood, Kent
to date	Assistant to Company Accountant

Peter's Brasserie is a large, busy wine bar and restaurant employing thirty-five full- and part- time staff. The company is privately owned. The work is varied and interesting, including:

- Initially running a complete set of manual accounts, e.g. cash book, sales and purchase ledger, banking, petty cash, bank reconciliations, VAT. Accuracy is vital with the large number of daily transactions.

- PAYE for all staff, including casual workers and directors. Improved the existing system by designing time sheets which staff now complete each week as opposed to monthly.

Page 2   **JOHN COLES**

- Producing accurate month-end figures for the directors to assist cash flow forecasting, and helping the Accountant in compiling final accounts, profit and loss and balance sheet.

- Deputising for the accountant and ensuring the department runs smoothly.

- Played a key role in successfully computerising the accounts using Sage software on Amstrad PC, which has allowed much swifter access to financial information.

Previous Employment

Sept 1984 to August 1987	DCC Ltd, Orpington, Kent Accounts Supervisor (1985 – 1987) Accounts Assistant (1984 – 1985)

DCC Ltd is a large engineering firm producing extrusion instruments for the plastics industry. During three enjoyable years here, in which time I was promoted, responsibilities included:

- Supervising the sales and bought ledger clerk, calculating VAT, collection of time sheets, banking and petty cash. Assisted on payroll during staff holidays, where I learned several aspects of PAYE and NI.

- Calculating costings on non-standard products and providing quotes on parts for the factory manager.

- Compiling monthly sales figures from ledgers and presenting these to the accountant in report form.

- Dealing with customers or suppliers who visited or telephoned with accounts queries, and ensuring that they were helped as quickly and efficiently as possible.

Skills

Computer software experience: Pegasus and Sage packages and some exposure to WordPerfect and Ability. IBM PCs used for over 3 years.

Full, clean driving licence held since June 1991 (car owner)

Achievements

I coach football every Saturday for the East Kent Juniors, who have won ten games this season, and was awarded 'Employee of the Month' in June 1986 at DCC for investigating and correcting a large error on a key customer account.

Personal and work references are available upon request

CURRICULUM VITAE

Ben Stevens
7 Inglewood Road, Forest Hill, London. SE23 2TS
Tel. 0181-291 5534

Employment History

June 1974 -   **HARTGATE DISTRIBUTION LTD, Peckham**
May 1995

Senior Fax and Copier Engineer	(1983 — 1995)
Fax Engineer	(1979 — 1983)
Copier Engineer	(1978 — 1979)
Workshop Technician	(1974 — 1978)

Hartgate Distribution Ltd is an office equipment dealer, specialising in photocopier and facsimile machines. Working throughout Central and South London as Senior Engineer in a small team of Technicians/Engineers, responsibilities included:

- Servicing a wide range of photocopier and fax machines and solving any malfunctions which occurred.

- Maintaining accurate records of all work carried out; planning and organising daily calls in order to make efficient use of time and minimise travel costs.

- Building up good working relationships with customers and diffusing any potentially difficult situations.

- Deputising for the Area Manager and organising regular engineering team meetings to share ideas and information, helping to create a motivated workforce.

- Working closely with management, other field staff, despatch organisers (who received customer calls for service) and customers in order to ensure the smooth running of the service division.

Product Presentation – Your CV

- Promoted to Senior Fax and Copier Engineer following recommendation from the Area Manager.

- Prior to working in Field Service, spent four years in the Workshop which developed both technical and product knowledge with particular respect to problem-solving.

1968—1974   **GPO TELECOMMUNICATIONS, West Norwood**
Installer   (1973 — 1974)
Wireman and Tester   (1968 — 1973)

Promoted up from Wireman and Tester to Installer, where responsibilities included: distribution of workload for up to twenty staff on site; liaison with Head Office to report progress; ensuring project ran smoothly and on schedule; management of staff time sheets and payment of hourly paid staff.

1961—1968   **GPO CITY, Central London**
Telephone Technician

Worked throughout Central London as a Technician, installing telephones in homes and businesses.

1959—1961   Two years in the Army.

Training   Numerous fax and photocopier courses (internal) for Ricoh, Infotec, Canon.
Team Development Course 1979. Customer Service Course 1980.
Colour copier course 1991.

Other Information   Date of Birth: 4/10/41
Full, clean driving licence
British nationality
Married, 4 adult children.
Educated at Charlton Park Secondary School, Peckham.

Full references are available on request.

Jane Thomas
61 Mount Ephraim Road, Brighton, East Sussex. BN24 OND
Tel: 01273-03804

Profile

An experienced Marketing Manager with a wide variety of skills, and a proven track record in business development. In-depth knowledge of FMCG products within the toiletries sector and a successful track record in product management, strategic planning, market research and sales promotional activities. A versatile, articulate achiever with strong creative, analytical and people skills.

Significant Accomplishments

- Creative marketing tactics achieved and continued an impressive sales record in the UK despite effects of the recession. Profits maintained for three successive years.

- Played a key role in the acquisition by Pharmaco of 34 Mentis stores during 1988. Hands-on role in integrating existing marketing support staff by reorganising team to maximise their involvement, and by recruiting and training new staff as required.

Career History

1985 – March 95   PHARMACO PLC, Sussex

Pharmaco is one of the UK's leading retailers of toiletries products, exclusively selling own-brand, competitively priced goods.

Marketing Manager   (1988 – 95)
Assistant to Marketing Manager   (1985 – 88)

- A member of the Senior Marketing Team, heading a team of five staff in the provision of marketing and sales support services for 90 retail outlets, generating a total revenue of £102m.

- Working closely with the Marketing Director to develop key marketing strategies, which includes the establishment of standard product plans, regular research and communication programmes.

- Increasing sales efficiency across the entire product range by producing commercially oriented promotional brochures, customised communications literature, competitor and market information.

- Initiating marketing strategies which include monitoring competitors' activity, targeting specific towns for additional promotional campaigns and monitoring the results.

- Accurate planning, positioning and pricing of six new product lines which resulted in successful launch and projected sales of £300,000 in 1991. Closely involved in the selection of new advertising agency.

- Promoted to the position of Manager following key contribution in the Mentis acquisition.

Training Courses

Managing the Marketing Function; Marketing in the Retail Sector –
    The Chartered Institute of Marketing (1989)
Business Development; Team Leadership – Hartley Ltd (1988)
Finance for Non-Financial Managers; Sales Management –
    Crandhurst Training (1987)

1984 – 85

Took a year out following university to travel. Visited the Far East and Australia.

Education

1981 – 84	BSc (Hons) Business Studies 2.1
Sussex University	
1976 – 81	2 'S' levels (English, History)
Brighton Grammar School	3 GCE 'A' levels: Business Studies (B); Economics (C), English (C) 10 GCE 'O' levels

Other Information
    Date of Birth: 23/12/ 1965.
    Married with one child aged five. Clean and full current driving licence.
    PC skills include Lotus 123, (Ami-Pro) database and WordPerfect 5.1.
    Leisure pursuits include tennis, squash, athletics and golf.

CURRICULUM VITAE

Personal Details

Ann Powell
Flat 11, Highfields House
Summer Road, Enfield, Middlesex
EN4 2HG
0181-704 9932

D.O.B: 14.03.1967

Nationality: British

Status: Married

Career History

Aug. 1989	Parkway Assurance Plc, Enfield	
to Mar. 1995	Senior Pensions Administrator	(1990 – 1995)
	Pensions Administrator	(1989 – 1990)

As a Senior Pensions Administrator (promoted in 1990), supervising three clerks, my responsibilities included:

- Servicing and thoroughly checking individual and group pension policies, i.e. alterations, lapses, revivals and paid-up policies. These required thorough checking and it was important to ensure that all documentation was accurate.

- Transfers – calculating exact transfer values, liaising with and payment to policyholders and helping them with queries and dealing with other insurance companies.

- Administration of new Executive Retirement Benefit Schemes. These schemes operated under different rules, hence it was also my responsibility to train and assist the junior staff. I ran a two-day staff workshop when these were launched.

- Liaising with district offices, insurance companies, banks, building societies, financial institutions and investigating accounts queries. I helped to set up a new computerised Query System which reduced investigation times by two days.

- Using Pace Insurance software for documentation and databases, Lotus 1-2-3 and Sage for calculations on transfers and WordPerfect 5.1 for word-processing.

Jul. 1986   **General Bank Plc**
to Jul. 1987   **Cashier (Grade II)**

As Cashier in this major high street Bank, my responsibilities included:

- Corporate and personal counter duties and dealing helpfully with all customer queries and transactions such as entering cheque and giro credit details on the computer; issuing statements and promptly despatching cheques for clearing. Also ensuring that the till balanced at the end of each working day. I won four awards for Cashier of the Month during my year here.

Education

1978 – 1983   Educated in Jamaica where I attained Leaving Certificate in 7 subjects

1983 – 1985   Manchester Regional College
2 GCE 'A' levels: Economics and English. RSA Typing Stage I & II

1987 – 1989   Harrow Polytechnic
BTEC National Certificate in Business & Finance

1995   Currently taking evening classes in advanced WP skills (Windows)

Interests   Swimming (twice a week), reading and playing the piano.

Below is a comprehensive checklist you can use to format your own CV.

CV Details

Full name ....
Address ....
....
....
....

Telephone (H) ....(W)..........................
Nationality ....
Date of birth ....
Marital status ....

School education (Secondary, from age 11)

Date from	To	Name of school
....	....	....
....	....	....
....	....	....
....	....	....

Examination results

Date	Type (e.g. GCSE/CSE/O & A)	Subject	Grade
....	....	....	....
....	....	....	....
....	....	....	....
....	....	....	....
....	....	....	....
....	....	....	....
....	....	....	....
....	....	....	....
....	....	....	....
....	....	....	....

Any awards/positions of responsibility
....
....
....
....
....

Product Presentation – Your CV

College/higher education (including part time or evening class and professional studies)

Date from   To   Name and address of college

....
....
....
....

Qualifications

Date   Type (e.g. HNC/OND)   Course/Subject   Grade

....
....
....
....
....

Other courses attended (e.g. WP, computers, sales, HGV, customer service)
Date from   To   Course/subject   Name of institution

....
....
....
....
....

Other information
Driving licence (status and date passed)...
Languages..
Computers and software used..
....
....
....
Typing speed ....Shorthand speed..............................
Other (a) ....
Other (b) ....

Interests..
....
....
....

EMPLOYMENT HISTORY

Current or last employment

Company nameDates fromToSize/location
....

Position (s)Reporting toSupervising whomDepartment
....
....
....

Brief description of company
....
....
....

What duties/responsibilities and what each one achieved on a day-to-day basis

1. ....
....
....

2. ....
....
....

3. ....
....
....

4. ....
....
....

5. ....
....
....

6. ....
....
....

7. ....
....
....
8. ....
....
....
9. ....
....
....
10. ....
....
....

Any special projects and/or achievements? What particular skills did you use in this job?

1. ....
....
....
2. ....
....
....
3. ....
....
....
4. ....
....
....

Any other details? (e.g. promotions)
....
....
....

Reason for leaving
....
....
....

Previous employment 1 or (previous job if same company)

Company name   Dates from   To   Size/location
....

Position (s)   Reporting to   Supervising whom   Department
....
....

Brief description of company
....
....

What duties/responsibilities and what each one achieved on a day-to-day basis

1. ....
   ....
2. ....
   ....
3. ....
   ....
4. ....
   ....
5. ....
   ....

Any special projects and/or achievements? What particular skills did you use in this job?

1. ....
   ....
2. ....
   ....

Any other details?
....
....

Previous employment 2

Company name   Dates from   To   Size/location
....

Position (s)   Reporting to   Supervising whom   Department
....

Brief description of company
....
....

What duties/responsibilities and what each one achieved on a day-to-day basis

1. ....
   ....
2. ....
   ....
3. ....
   ....
4. ....
   ....

Any special projects and/or achievements? What particular skills did you use in this job?

1. ....
   ....
2. ....
   ....

Any other details?
....
....
....

Previous employment 3

Company name   Dates from   To   Size/location
....

Position (s)   Reporting to   Supervising whom   Department
....

Brief description of company
....
....

What duties/responsibilities and what each one achieved on a day-to-day basis
1. ....
....
2. ....
....
3. ....
....

Any special projects and/or achievements? What particular skills did you use in this job?
1. ....
....
2. ....
....

Any other details?
....
....
....
....

Previous employment 4

Company name   Dates from   To   Size/location
....

Position (s)   Reporting to   Supervising whom   Department
....

Brief description of company
....
....

What duties/responsibilities and what each one achieved on a day-to-day basis

1. ....
....

2. ....
....

3. ....
....

Any special projects and/or achievements? What particular skills did you use in this job?

1. ....
....

2. ....
....

Any other details?
....
....
....
....

Previous employment 5

Company name   Dates from   To   Size/location
....

Position (s)   Reporting to   Supervising whom   Department
....

Brief description of company
....
....
....

What duties/responsibilities and what each one achieved on a day-to-day basis
1. ....
....
2. ....
....

Any special projects and/or achievements? What particular skills did you use in this job?
1. ....
....
2. ....
....

Any other details?
....
....
....
....

Other previous employers (continue in the same way if you need to):

Profile or Resumé (if desired)

Use this space to write your own 'snapshot'. Although this will eventually go at the beginning of your CV, do this profile last as it's much easier when you have all the facts down.

✎ ....
....
....
....
....
....
....
....
....
....
....
....
....
....
....
....
....
....
....
....
....
....
....
....
....
....
....
....
....

For detailed advice and examples of CVs, read *Sure-Hire Resumés* by Robbie Kaplan (Amacom Books, distributed in Europe by Management Books 2000).

5. THE TARGET MARKET -

Who Will Buy Me? How And Where Will I Find Them?

Vacancies

There are several sources of vacancies, and people rarely try all of them, often only using agencies and newspaper advertisements. Consequently they miss out on good, relevant opportunities. If you want to maximise your chances of success be as thorough as possible in your approach.

Research

A key factor to success in your job search is researching potential employers. Whether you are exploring an area of particular interest or have found a specific vacancy, thorough research will help you to find out more about the company and the industry. The marketing manager would make sure he knew his potential buyers before he wasted time and money on a huge mailshot to the whole world!

If you are carrying out general research to find out where job opportunities may lie, you can research companies by sector, product, location and size. The best way to start is to take your first two priorities in terms of ideal jobs and concentrate on those, otherwise it can seem a daunting task. This chapter gives some ideas about specific research. There are also the following places you can use:

Libraries

Your own local public library and any business or college libraries are good places to start. Not only will a visit to the library get you out of the house, but it will help you to concentrate and channel your job-searching activities. Libraries are also free.

If you know the name of the company you are researching, a telephone call to the reference section can save you a lot of legwork. Librarians are a mine of information and can save you a lot of time in your research by pointing you to the right reference books.

Chambers of Commerce

One problem with most reference books is that companies have to be fairly big to get a listing. However, your local Chamber of Commerce will have information about local companies (as long as they are COC members). They will also sell you detailed lists but they charge about £70 for 200 names. As a last resort and if other free sources of information have been exhausted, this can be a worthwhile investment, particularly if you are swapping information with other job seekers.

Newspapers, periodicals and media

National, local and trade papers can tell you about company activities, trends and so forth. By reading general articles and advertisements for jobs other than your desired job, you can glean a lot of information about what the companies are up to. For example, they may be opening a new department, site or division, they may have won a major contract that will soon need extra staff, or they may be moving into new product areas where your skills could be useful.

Vacancies

National newspapers. National newspapers usually carry high-quality vacancies, but the disadvantage is that the response they get is often extremely large. So if you are applying for a vacancy where you are not a really good match, the odds may be rather against your getting a positive response. However, do not be deterred where you are a good fit for the job. Some national newspapers have features which can be useful: for instance, the *Daily Mail* has 'Career Link' – their computer will search out all the vacancies recently advertised in the paper (ring free on 0800-774488). The vacancies are also sent to Teletext each week. As it can be expensive to buy all the newspapers every day, you could use the library, share newspapers with other job seekers, or just buy the papers on the day in which your profession/industry advertises. At the end of this section you will find a chart showing the advertising schedules of the major papers as of June 1994.

Local newspapers. Your local newspaper could be of help if you wish to find a job close to home. Most publishers do different papers for different regions, but many of the jobs are advertised in all the issues. The rule should be that if a paper covers a region you can work in, buy it regularly, irrespective of where you live. The papers you pay for usually carry more (and often better) job advertisements than free ones.

Trade press. The trade press are an excellent source of relevant vacancies and a way of finding out about the activities of companies operating in that particular industry. Most industries have a variety of trade publications, from Accounting to Wines & Spirits. Details can be found in BRAD (British Research and Data) in your library. Your library may be able to obtain a copy of a particular publication if you ask.

Job papers. There has been a growth in job papers over the past year or so. The quality varies but it's always worth getting hold of a copy as soon as they come out – your library or Job Centre should stock them. You have to be very quick as jobs often get filled almost within days of the advert appearing. The adverts are usually free to employers with vacancies; you pay around 60p – £1 for each paper.

Radio advertisements. Local radio stations often have advertisements for vacancies. Large local employers find it a very effective way of reaching local people. The type of vacancy varies although it is usually sales or retail. They may also have a careers information service (e.g. Capital Radio Careers Helpline).

Television. Some television stations list job and training opportunities, through Oracle, Ceefax or Teletext. Specialised career and job programmes are usually on a Sunday morning.

Employment Agencies and Recruitment Consultancies

Research

Choose an employment agency with a good reputation for recruitment in your field. You can sort out which ones by studying the trade press and seeing what type of jobs they are advertising. The particular job they are advertising may not be right for you, but the chances are that they may have others in that sector.

You can also ask friends or colleagues or the personnel staff of your company (as long as they know you are leaving or you have already left, preferably on good terms!) if they can recommend any to you. There is an annual directory called *The Executive Grapevine* which lists the larger search and selection consultancies. You should be able to find a copy in your library.

Otherwise, there are several pages of employment agencies and recruitment consultancies in the telephone books. Ring a few and see what sort of response you get. If they sound professional and knowledgeable about your industry or profession, they may be able to help you.

Vacancies

Only about 15-20 per cent of vacancies are filled through agencies, so it is unwise to concentrate all your activities just in this area. In the current economic climate, recruitment agencies and consultancies are having a tough time, as many companies are doing their own recruitment to save on fees, and if people are writing in directly their details are often kept on file. It is worth bearing this in mind, as you may get a very negative and false picture of the job market from agencies: they are only seeing things from one angle.

Employment agencies/recruitment consultancies vary in the type of actual work they will take on. There are three main ways in which they work for their clients, although some do a mixture of all or use two of these methods to find the right people.

Register agencies. These handle the majority of junior to mid-level vacancies (e.g. £5,000 to £30,000). Ordinary recruitment consultants as well as 'High Street' agencies fall into this category. They have a large database of candidates and vacancies and either advertise for candidates at their own expense or search their files for suitable people when they get a vacancy in. They may deal only in a certain type of candidate or industry. There are a large number of agencies that handle general vacancies, but the quality of the service varies very widely.

Selection consultancies. They take a position from the company and advertise the vacancy on their behalf. The consultancy filters the responses, interviews a limited number of applicants, and then presents a shortlist to the client for their final approval. Many of these consultancies operate a database system too, so they may be worth contacting to see if they retain details of people with your experience.

Search consultancies ('Headhunters'). These take a position from the company, research other companies to find the right person and then approach that person directly. The vacancy is not usually advertised. This type of recruitment is normally carried out for more senior executives.

Getting the best out of agencies/consultancies and their services

Good recruitment consultants really are worth their weight in gold – they can be helpful, supportive, professional and interested in you. A poor one may not treat you with the same levels of respect or care and attention, so do choose who you use carefully. After all, they are in a way representing you in your job search.

If an agency refuses to see you but tells you to send your CV in for their files, it is usually better to move on to the next one. You need to meet them to tell them what you want and to sell yourself. You also need to find out how they work: will they send your CV out without your permission or will they ring you first to see if you are actually interested in the job? Do they want you to ring them on a regular basis (preferably they do, every 10 days or so)? It is up to you to keep in touch with them to let them know that you are still looking.

One word of warning: agencies and consultancies are not allowed by law to charge you a fee for placing you in a job. The client (the company with the vacancy) must always pay the fee. If they ask for money, do not pay (you can even report them to the Department of Employment) and move onto another one. Some may charge you a fee for preparing your CV, which is perfectly legal and a good idea if you have no one else who can type. They may also offer you interview skills training or help with letters and so forth, which again is legal and a good idea if you need help.

Trade Associations and Professional Institutions

Research

Trade associations can provide a lot of information about a particular company in their sector. A directory, *Trade Associations and Professional Bodies of the UK*, gives names, addresses and telephone numbers of all of these and can be found in a good business library. Ring the relevant one and ask for the general information department or library.

Trade fairs (or annual trade conventions) are a useful way of meeting people and companies and finding out about activities. Look in your trade press for details of relevant ones coming up.

Vacancies

Many trade associations/professional institutions run a free vacancy service for members (as well as advice on training and upgrading your skills). If you are in a recognised profession – for example, credit management, accounting, freight forwarding, transport, etc. – then it is worth joining the institute if you are not already a member. They may also be able to give you a list of their company (corporate) members, which can be useful in making speculative (i.e. 'cold') applications to companies.

Job Centres

Research

Your local Job Centre stocks a series of booklets designed to help you with your job search, such as CV writing and improving your interview technique. In addition to this, they have details of Government-funded training schemes designed for the long-term unemployed. They are not, however, able to give careers guidance.

Vacancies

Job Centres handle a wide range and number of job vacancies. Not all of them will necessarily have the type of job you are seeking, as they tend to carry fairly local and sometimes a large proportion of very junior level vacancies, but it is worth a visit to your local one to find out. The service is free to both employer and candidate. They are run by Central Government and are often attached to local UB40 offices. They display 'Job Cards' through which you can browse. Select the jobs which appeal to you and one of the assistants will try to arrange an interview.

Jobs change regularly so it is worth visiting them two or three times a week if they seem to carry your type of vacancy. Although Job Centres keep in touch with others in the area about job opportunities, it is much better to go to all the local ones yourself.

'Dial a Job' is a service run by the Department of Employment in conjunction with the Greater London Job Centres who notify them of all their vacancies. If you phone 0171-287 0100 during office hours they will do a search on computer, and if they have a vacancy that interests you they will try to arrange an interview. The service is free, except for the cost of the call.

Many Job Centres also run their own **Job Club,** and in some areas make it compulsory for unemployed people claiming benefits for more than three months to attend. There is at the moment a waiting list in many areas so it is wise to get yourself on the list as soon as possible.

The Job Clubs are a good way of motivating yourself to get out of the house, you have free use of their telephones, they will help you with letters and interviews, postage and stationery costs are paid for by them and they have large databases of local employers.

Forming your own Job Club with other people looking for work is an excellent way of swapping vacancy details if you come across vacancies in which you are not interested, information about companies, names and contacts and so forth. It also provides you with some support throughout your job search.

Job Fairs

Job Fairs are not quite as popular as they were a few years ago, mainly because they are organised for employment in particular industries where the recruitment of staff is difficult (usually due to a skills shortage). For example, before computers became so widely used there were very few specialists on the market, so employers had to work harder to attract the right people.

There are not the same levels of skills shortages at the moment, but even in today's tough employment market Job Fairs for skilled personnel are still a good way for employers to reach a large number of people and show them the company and its products.

A typical Job Fair is held in a hotel or large hall; several companies will have their own representatives and personnel managers present on their own stand, with the aim of providing careers information to candidates in an informal setting. From the job seeker's point of view there are three golden rules:

- Dress exactly as you would do for an ordinary, formal interview.
- Take along plenty of copies of your CV.
- Treat every conversation you have with the company representatives as if it were a interview. Do not be fooled by the informal setting: they are there to judge you just as much as you are there to judge them.

If a company takes your name and address with the view of contacting you to arrange a formal interview, make a note of the company representative's name. You can drop them a line after the Job Fair saying it was a pleasure to meet them and hope that you may have the opportunity of doing so again. It shows that you are interested and professional.

Companies

Research

You can research companies by industry, products or services, company size and location, by using your local library. The librarian will show you how to use the directories of company information. They will contain the basic facts you need to identify the types of company for which you would like to work.

Most companies will have literature or a brochure or, if they are a public company, a set of accounts that the general public has the right to see. If the company is medium to large, you can ask one of several departments – Marketing, Public Relations, Research & Development or Personnel – for some general literature. For smaller companies, you could ask Personnel, Sales or even a friendly switchboard operator to send some details to you. You are not asking for a job – just information at this stage (see the section on telephone applications later).

Vacancies

The vast majority of vacancies (it has been said 75 per cent) are neither advertised nor registered with employment agencies. It is a fair assumption to make, therefore, that many companies may have a suitable job about which you are unaware. Many people have found that a job was about to be advertised, or the company was simply thinking about creating a vacancy and had not decided on taking any actual action. The fact that a suitable CV landed on someone's desk at the right time made them the first candidate to be considered.

The best way of uncovering these 'hidden' jobs is to write 'speculative' letters enclosing a copy of your CV to companies for whom you would like to work. It is clearly a waste of time writing to a company that does not employ people in your profession or field. It is also important to tell that company in your letter why you are applying to them as opposed to any other (even though you will be writing to several).

Some companies (usually factories and shops) also have a notice-board of vacancies in or outside their premises. If you are seeking this type of work, a visit round the local shopping centre/industrial estate can certainly pay off. Go dressed as if you were attending an interview – everyone you talk to, including the receptionist, will form an initial impression of you. You might even be given an interview on the spot if the business is a small one.

Friends and Contacts ('Networking' or 'Word of Mouth')

Networking is becoming the most successful way of finding employment. In a survey in 1992, 55 per cent of unemployed people who obtained work within 14 weeks did so through networking (which shows just how many jobs never get advertised).

Networking is *not* about directly asking your friends for a specific job; it is simply talking to your friends and contacts for ideas to find people who may know of opportunities where your skills and experience could be utilised.

Research

You may know a lot or perhaps just a few people, either socially or through previous work. Draw up a list of people you have had a good relationship with over the past few years. Divide them into categories if this would be helpful, such as 'Business Suppliers', 'Competitors' (see below), and you will be surprised at how many people you really do know. Networking is rather like a family tree – you start off with one person, who leads you onto two people, who lead onto six, who lead onto ten, and so on.

If you are looking for employment in a field where you know someone, ask them about their industry. They may know of companies you have never heard of, and they can give you valuable information about specific companies. But do not let them bias your view about a company – even if they say that their products are rotten or that a manager there is difficult to get on with or useless at the job. Let yourself be the judge of that! We do not all have the same ideas about what is a good or bad company or employee.

Making contact

When you start your networking, there will be obviously some people you know better than others, so contact those first to get you into the right frame of mind. People *will* help you: put yourself in their place – if someone asked you for a little advice, wouldn't you be willing to spend a few minutes with them?

Again, remember you are not directly asking for a job – people can feel pushed into a corner if you do so. Just ask for advice: say you have an interest in a particular field and that you are looking for information. Ask if they would be prepared to spend just half an hour with you. Before you contact or meet them, spend some time preparing what you what to ask them. They may have no vacancies but might suggest that you contact someone else in the same field who could be helpful too.

If you do get the name of someone to contact, ask the person who gave you the name if they would mind calling them on your behalf to introduce you. If you find this difficult, at least ask that person if you can use their name to break the ice.

When you have had a meeting, do write and thank the person for seeing you. It will keep you in their mind and you could get more contacts. If one of their referrals leads to a job, again, let them know and thank them for their help.

Networking – Who Do You Know Who Would Talk to You?

I am are not suggesting that you should contact every single person on the list below – they might not be people that you know at all. However, even though you may feel there is little point in talking to your bank manager if you are a hairdresser, you never know – he might have been speaking to another of his customers last week who runs a salon! This list is intended to give you an idea of where to start and will also show you just how many people there are that could give you a lead to a job – full or part-time, in your field or any other. Write in the names of people that you could contact:

Source	Name
Ex-colleagues	
Ex-employers	
Competitor companies	
Competitor employees	
Companies next door	
Companies on same estate	
People in office block	
Partners' work colleagues	
Neighbours	
Relatives	
People you know socially	
People you play sports with	
College/school friends	
Teachers	
Plumber/electrician	
Decorator	
Garage owner	
Hairdresser/barber	
Bank manager/solicitor	
Building society manager	
Financial adviser	
Accountant	
Local shopkeepers	
Church friends	
Local restaurants/pub	
Hotel staff or owners	
Others	

The Target Market – Who Will Buy Me?

Now that you have all the information you need to start your job search, you can begin to draw up your action plan. You may have a list of several possible job options which can be ranked in order of preference and worked through individually, or a general one, as shown over the page. This is followed by a blank that you can copy.

The Job Search Manual

ACTION PLAN

John Coles
Week: One   **Date:** 22 January 1995

Activity	Which, who, where, by when	Done or Next Action
Weekly activity target	30 activities in total – including spec. letters, calls, contacts, applications and agencies	
Newspapers and trade press	*Evening Standard* each night, especially Thurs. *Surrey Advertiser* on Friday *Croydon Times* on Monday *Bromley Gazette* on Tuesday *New Accountant* – visit library on Tuesday *Hotel and Caterer* – Thursday	✓ Get a copy from Peter ✓ ✓ ✓
Networking	Contact Clive Parker at Green Bros. Call Jenny Andrews from Dad's firm Drop in and see Fred at Jones & Co. Anne to ask her Personnel Manager about any vacancies Speak to Alan at football club re his contacts at Blake's Wine Bar	✓ ✓ ✓ ✓ – he says write in ✓ – nothing at mo.
Agencies	Contact AllVacs Ltd to arrange an interview Call Jean Ash at Staff Resources International Register with Accounting Solutions Register with Bookkeepers Unlimited Call Financial Placements Call Johnson Staff Ltd Speak to John Smith re agencies he used last year	✓ – see record chart ✓ – see record chart ✓ – see record chart ✓ – see record chart Call next week – on hols at mo.
Speculative	Visit library on Monday to research hotels and restaurants in London, Croydon, Bromley and Beckenham. Write two letters each day to these: Mon Tues Wed Thurs Fri	✓ – twenty names found ✓ ✓ ✓
Other	Find *Hotel & Catering Yearbook* – try Croydon Library Letter to Mr Thomson thanking him for meeting Stamps from Post Office. More stationery Check with Mike Davison re being my referee Find out about Government Career Development Loan for computer course at Sanders Training	No, try Bromley ✓ ✓ Office only open 2 – 3.30 pm

The Target Market – Who Will Buy Me?

ACTION PLAN

Week: **Date:**

Activity   *Which, who, where, by when*   *Done or Next Action*

Weekly activity
target

Newspapers and
trade press

Networking

Agencies

Speculative

Other

ALTERNATIVE MARKETS

Having worked through this far, you may have come up with some alternatives – whether that be changing career entirely, retraining, returning to education, taking a part-time job or setting up your own business. A major change requires thorough research so that you can make sensible, informed decisions. Here are some starting points.

Career change

Every local authority has at least one Careers Centre, with a library, information on a wide range of occupations, education courses and training options, usually with a section devoted entirely to the needs of adults. Some Careers Centres offer free career guidance facilities to adults. You will find your nearest one listed in the telephone directory.

A good book that will give you some ideas is *The Penguin Careers Guide* – published by Penguin. This gives details of over 300 occupations, the qualifications, learning opportunities, etc. You will find it in most libraries.

Retraining or studying

Learning a new skill or gaining a qualification can enhance your career prospects substantially. Some professions require you to pass exams so you do need to find out the costs, the time frame and the sacrifices you will have to make while you are retraining or studying. Either can usually be done on a full- or part-time basis or distance learning. Depending on the area you wish to pursue, in addition to the Careers Service you can contact:

- The National Association for Education and Guidance Services for Adults works within some local authorities and is free. Ask for details at your local library who may have the *Educational Guidance Services for Adults*, a directory of members.
- Your local further education college (see Yellow Pages) for academic, professional, technical or general interest courses.
- Higher educational establishments (universities and what used to be called polytechnics) for vocational or academic courses. For distance learning at degree level contact the Open University on 01908-274066.
- Private training companies for short or medium-term courses (e.g. computing, typing or accounting). See your local press or look in Yellow Pages under 'Training'.

- Trade associations or institutions for seminars or short courses.
- Training and Enterprise Councils. Run by the Department of Employment, the 82 TECs work with other business organisations to offer a wide range of services, including information and advice about training for a new job, adding to your existing skills or starting or expanding your own business. See Yellow Pages or ask at your Job Centre for details.

Part-time or temporary work

This can have several advantages whilst you are considering your future and long-term career:

- You can try out a new job or career before committing yourself entirely.
- You can learn a new skill that will add to your experience and your CV.
- It can often turn into a full-time, long-term career if you prove yourself to be hard-working and capable. When a full-time job does arise within the company, you may be one of the first to hear about it and therefore will have the advantage over other job seekers.
- You can generate income whilst you are seeking full-time or long-term work.
- Being in a job usually improves your morale and gets you out of the house!

There are, however, a couple of disadvantages:

- You may be so busy that you have no time to continue with your proper job search campaign – thus you may miss out on opportunities or be unable to attend interviews.
- When money is coming in, it is very easy to put the urgency of a job search to the back of your mind. You may find yourself in a rut if the job has no opportunity for you to develop your career, or if any experience you gain is not really going to be useful to you in the future.

Starting your own business or becoming self-employed

Banks. Information and advice is given by most clearing banks which often have a small business adviser. It is useful to obtain their information packs before you start talking directly to them, thus ensuring that when you do meet them you know what to discuss.

Advice for Small Businesses. There is a scheme (previously known as the Small Firms Service) which is privately run but supported through the Training and Enterprise Council (TEC). If you ring 100 and ask for 'Freefone Enterprise' you will be referred to a freephone number for your nearest Business Centre. The one for London is the Greater London Business Centre (Tel. 0800-222 999).

Business Start-Up (previously 'Enterprise Allowance Scheme'). This is run differently by each of the local TECs (see page 73). The scheme provides £40-50 per week for up to six months to help you get started. The criteria for eligibility vary within each TEC, but generally speaking you need to have been unemployed (usually for six weeks), 18-65 years old and have up to £1,000 to invest. Access to free business counselling, help with preparing a business plan, general advice and training are available. Enquire at your local Job Centre and they will refer you to the appropriate TEC. You may lose unemployment benefit and possible income support if you are getting funds from this scheme.

Lawyers for Enterprise. This is an initiative from The Law Society where some lawyers will give one hour's free consultation about the legal aspects of your business. Telephone 0171-405 9075 and you will be sent a list of lawyers operating the scheme in your area.

Recommended reading on working for yourself:

Starting A Business On A Shoestring – published by Penguin Books.
Working For Yourself (a series on many businesses) – published by Kogan Page.
Starting A Small Business – published by Letts (a Royal Bank of Scotland book).
Running Your Own Business – published by Management Books 2000 (includes free update service).
The New Venture Handbook – Amacom Books, distributed by Management Books 2000.

Useful Reference Books for All Your Research

The Personnel Manager's Yearbook, published annually by AP Information Services. This gives details of the sector and size of practically every medium to large UK company or organisation (and any subsidiaries or overseas locations) with personnel and senior management names. It also has lists of trade organisations, consultancies and agencies such as recruitment, management and training and pensions. There is also a useful annual salary survey.

Kompass, published annually by Reed Information Services Ltd. This comes in three volumes and gives a country by country industrial listing of all companies within a geographical location, products, services and key managers. Most libraries will stock UK listings and the librarian or publishers will be able to advise you on foreign listings.

Key British Enterprises, published annually by Dunn & Bradstreet Ltd. A five-volume set, giving details of the products, services and size of Britain's top 20,000 companies.

The Executive Grapevine, published annually by Executive Grapevine International. A directory of recruitment consultancies dealing in middle and senior management positions. It indexes consultancies by job function and business sector and gives details of any overseas offices or connections.

Trade Associations and Professional Bodies of the UK, published annually by Gale Research. Lists details, names and addresses of all institutions and professional bodies.

BRAD (British Research and Data), published by Maclean Hunter. Used by the advertising industry this gives 'rate cards', i.e. prices of advertising space. It is very useful for your job search in finding relevant trade press as well as giving a breakdown of all published media, including the publisher's name and the industry sector.

Kelly's Business Directory, published by Kelly's Directories. Provides a comprehensive listing of British companies.

Who Owns Whom published by Dunn & Bradstreet. If a company is owned by another or affiliated in some way, this book will be useful in finding out more about corporate ownership and operating similarities.

Handbook of Market Leaders, published by Extel Financial Ltd. A biannual publication showing market leaders by sector.

The Times Top 1,000 Companies, published by Times Books. A list of companies by sector, turnover, product and number of employees with names of chairman/chief executive or managing director.

List of Lists, published by Benns Business Information Services. Gives fairly detailed information on manufacturing and service industries.

Whitakers Almanac, published by J Whitaker & Sons Ltd. An annual directory giving addresses of societies, institutions, trade unions, industrial research associations, banks, newspapers and periodicals.

Top 3,000 Directories and Annuals, published by Alan Armstrong & Associates. A directory of directories and annual publications.

Directory of Directories, published by Thomas Skinner Directories. Lists almost 60,000 directors by name, qualifications, business sector and company address.

Current British Directories, published by CBD Research – an encyclopaedia of directories.

Computer Users Yearbook (and Software Users Yearbook), both published annually by VNU Business Publications. Four volumes for each yearbook giving computer equipment, service companies and IT consultancies.

Charities Digest and Voluntary Agencies Directory, both list major UK charities, with contact names and activities. Also gives the addresses of all Citizen's Advice Bureaux throughout the UK.

Market Surveys

Again, these should be available from business libraries and include:

Keynote. Annually produces over 200 surveys analysing trends and future prospects in specific markets.

Mintel. Monthly magazines which analyse five particular markets.

British Business. A weekly Department of Trade and Industry publication on UK market statistics.

Retail Business Monthly. Published by The Economist Intelligence Unit, covering specific retail markets.

The Marketing Pocket Book. Published by the Advertising Association covering demographic, media and consumer spending statistics.

NEWSPAPER ADVERTISEMENTS OF VACANCIES

Paper	Evening Standard	The Times	Independent	Financial Times	
Monday	Accountancy. Business Day appts. Education appts. Financial, Insurance and Banking. Medical and Health. Public and Community.	'La Creme' (senior Secretarial). Educational appts.	Computing. Engineering. Science and Technology		
Tuesday	Body, Health and Leisure. Education, Tuition and Training. Fashion, Design and Tailoring. Graduates and Achievers. Hotel and Catering. Retail and Sales. Secretarial. Security.	Legal.	Accountancy. Finance and Banking.		
Wednesday	Building and Maintenance. Computer Engineering. Media Sales. Media, Creative and Marketing.	'La Creme'. Media. Marketing.		Finance. Banking. 'Top Opportunities' Senior Management.	
Thursday	General Management. Hotel and Catering. Retail Management. Sales and Sales Management. Secretarial 'Elite'. Security.	General. Public Sector. 'La Creme' Accountancy. Finance. General Management.	Public Sector. Educational. General. Graduate. Charity. Housing.	Accounting.	
Friday		Computing/ Information Technology.	Legal.	International Edition – Reprints Wed/Thurs. appts.	
Saturday					
Sunday		General Executive (repeats of all Thursday's appts).	All weekly vacancies repeated in the Business Section.		

The Target Market – Who Will Buy Me?

The Guardian	The Observer	The Daily Telegraph	Daily Express	Daily Mail
Media/Creative. Marketing. Secretarial.				
Educational. International appts.			Hotel and Catering. Secretarial. Building and Construction. Education. General appts.	
Public Sector.			Sales. Sales Management.	
Computing. Science and Technology. Finance and Business. General. Graduates.		Public Sector. Computing. Engineering. Sales and Marketing. General. Educational.	Engineering. Technical. Computing. Retail. General	All areas of Recruitment – 'Career Mail' feature.
Environment. Conservation. Housing.				
Repeats of Monday and Thursday.				
	'Executive Portfolio'. Plus Education and Courses section.	Public Sector. Computing. Engineering. Sales and Marketing. General. Educational.		

LOCAL, TRADE OR JOB PAPERS

Paper					
Monday					
Tuesday					
Wednesday					
Thursday					
Friday					
Saturday					
Sunday					

The Target Market – Who Will Buy Me?

NETWORKING ACTIVITIES

Source and contact name	Date written to or spoken to on phone	Result – information or referrals	

The Target Market – Who Will Buy Me?

	Next Action	Result	Remarks/further action	Filed under...

SPECULATIVE LETTERS TO COMPANIES

Company and contact name	Source of company details	Date written to or spoken to on phone	

The Target Market – Who Will Buy Me?

	Result and/or date they replied	Date to follow up	Remarks/further action	Filed under...

RECRUITMENT AGENCIES

Agency name and consultant	Interview date or date CV sent	Date to follow up	

The Target Market – Who Will Buy Me?

	Result	Next follow up	Remarks/further action	Filed under...

JOB ADVERTISEMENTS

Source and date of advertisement	Company and contact name or agency	Reference number and job title	

The Target Market – Who Will Buy Me?

	Date they replied	Result	Remarks/further action	Filed under...

6. PRODUCT PRESENTATION

Covering Letters, Application Forms and Telephone Applications

Covering letters are those that you send with your CV or application form. Depending on your reason for writing, each type of letter will be different. For example, a letter applying for a specific job will be very different from one you write to companies to enquire about possible vacancies.

Your covering letter should be as carefully prepared and professional as your CV – there is little use in sending a beautiful 'brochure' with a poorly presented letter. The letter is your opportunity to say why you are writing and what it is you have to offer, and it is often the first contact you will have with the person. Scruffy, badly written letters that are too long or letters which are far too 'salesey' will be rejected immediately and your CV may get no more than a cursory glance.

Points to Remember

- 'AIDA' – Attention, Interest, Desire and Action.

- Always state what you can do for them – not what they can do for you. Be positive throughout, using words that sound enthusiastic.

- Keep the letter brief but punchy – it has to be as eye-catching as your CV.

- Use plain white or cream unlined paper, blue or black ink – never 'fancy' paper.

- Handwritten letters are fine, but can be laborious when you are writing several. If your writing is not clear, you may get rejected so it is wise to get them typed unless you have been asked to send in a handwritten letter – you could get a friend to help you.

- If you are writing by hand, never write in block capitals throughout the letter.

- If your own grammar and spelling are not good, get someone else to check the letter. One way to 'proof-read' is to read the letter backwards, word by word: the brain often expects to see something that would normally follow and when it does not, it may be missed. Reading backwards helps to overcome this.

- Letters to 'Dear Sir' or 'Dear Madam' should end 'Yours faithfully' and letters to a named person should end with 'Yours sincerely'. It is best to write to a named person whenever possible.

- Always end your letter on a positive note, e.g. 'I look forward to hearing from you' or 'I look forward to speaking with you personally'.

Letters to Advertised Vacancies

The letter should let the recipient know what job you are interested in, and, in addition, it should emphasise why *you* are the right person for the job and the company.

There is little point in writing about skills or experience that are irrelevant to the job – you *must* show that you have read the specification carefully and that you meet their requirements. This is just as important whether you are applying directly to the company or through an agency.

Apply for a job as soon as you see it advertised, and send it by first-class post to show that you are keen and 'on the ball'. If you wait a few days you may find that the job has been filled.

One rather cheeky trick if you have the telephone number of a company is to ring and ask them for the fax number and fax your letter and CV so that it gets there before anyone else's! If the advert says 'Write in for an application form', do just that. If you are asked to 'Apply in writing', you should send in your CV with a covering letter as usual.

Drafting your Letter

Having read the job specification, you will need to go through the advertisement to assess exactly what they are looking for and how you match their requirements. Obviously, there will be many occasions where your skills do not exactly match their requirements. If you are struggling to find enough 'matching points' this could of course mean that you cannot really do the job and, if you do apply, are likely to get rejected anyway.

Applying for jobs where you stand very little chance of being considered will lead to constant rejection and does no good to your morale, in addition to being a waste of your valuable time when you could be concentrating on other, more productive areas. The golden rule is that if you can do 65 per cent of the job and have the ability to learn how to do the rest, then it is certainly worth applying.

Underline the key features such as the responsibilities and the type of personality, experience, qualifications desired, etc. Then take a sheet of paper and draw a line down the middle. On the left-hand side make a list of all their requirements, and on the right-hand side write your relevant skills or experience.

For example, let us assume that Ann Powell, the lady whose CV was shown earlier, has seen the following advertisement:

Senior Life Policy Administrator   North London

As a leading name in Financial Services, Ashville Assurance Plc is improving and developing the standards of sales support and customer service. We now seek a Senior Life Policy Administrator for our Uxbridge Head Office. The successful applicant will have at least three years' experience in Life and/or Pensions Administration and a good understanding of legislation affecting policies and financial services. Some exposure to a Customer Care programme is desirable, and the role will involve working closely with the Senior Life Manager to build up a team of reliable and efficient staff.

Further training will be given where necessary, but ideal candidates will have used a variety of computerised systems and held a supervisory role. You should be aged between 25 and 30, have a good educational background (to at least O level), good communication skills both verbal and written, and be keen to advance your career in Financial Services. If you would like to be considered for this post, please write enclosing CV to Mrs J Morgan, Personnel Manager, Ashville Assurance plc, Braintree Rd, Uxbridge, Middlesex, UB12 8OJ.

Ann's matching exercise could look like this:

Requirements and specification — My skills/experience

Requirements and specification	My skills/experience
Improving and developing sales support and customer service	Helped on the Query system which reduced investigation times by two days. Six years' experience of dealing with customers.
Senior Life Policy Administrator	Pensions procedures are very similar.
Three years' experience in L and/or P	Three years' experience in Pensions.
Good understanding of legislation	Fully trained in LAUTRO rules and have trained others.
Working closely with the Senior Life Manager	Worked as part of the senior team with the Senior Pensions Manager.
Further training will be given	Keen to get more training.
Knowledge of computerised systems	Used IBM mainframe, Pace Insurance Software, Sage and Lotus 1-2-3.
Supervisory role	Promoted two years ago, now manage and train three staff.
Aged 25-30	Aged 25.
O levels – good education	Leaving Certificate and two A levels, plus BTEC.
Good communication skills	Used to dealing with difficult customers on the telephone and in writing and ensuring their problems are listened to and resolved. Also used to communicating with the team.

Ann's letter in response to the advertisement:

Mrs J Morgan
Personnel Manager
Ashville Assurance plc
Braintree Road
Uxbridge
Middlesex
UB12 8OJ

Flat 11, Highfields House
Summer Road
Enfield
Middlesex
EN4 2HG

Telephone: 0181-704 9932

4 April 1995

Dear Mrs Morgan,

Ref: Your advertisement (Evening Standard 3/4/95) – Senior Life Policy Administrator

I would very much like to be considered for the above post for your Uxbridge Head Office.

Having spent three years in Policy Administration with Parkway Assurance, the latter two as a Senior/Supervisor in the Pensions area, I have hands-on experience of improving sales support and customer service – in particular, ensuring that clients' queries are resolved promptly, as I was involved in a project where we reduced investigation times by two days. Dealing with customers and working in a team has been invaluable in improving my written and verbal communication skills.

I am well versed in LAUTRO legislation, and have worked closely with my Senior Pensions Manager on developing and training the staff, both on a day-to-day basis and running in-house workshops.

I have been trained in several aspects of computer systems, including specialised insurance software, and am most interested in undertaking further training.

I have a high degree of self-motivation, which resulted in my receiving promotion last year. I have two GCE A levels and a BTEC in Business and Finance, and am aged 25 years.

I enclose my Curriculum Vitae for your consideration and would very much welcome the opportunity to discuss my application with you in person. I look forward to hearing from you in the near future.

Yours sincerely,

Ann Powell
Enc.

Letters to Advertised Vacancies Where Minimal Information Is Given

Not all job advertisements will be as detailed as the one shown on page 92. This can make the matching exercise difficult. You need to use your imagination if the advert does not list their requirements or gives little detail about the company.

You can telephone the company (if a telephone number is provided) and say that you are interested to find out more about their requirements for the vacancy. You may be able to speak directly to the person who is handling the vacancy; you need to have your CV to hand when you make the call in case you are asked questions about your experience. It is *vital* to prepare a brief list of the points you would like to raise. Approaching the company in this way will certainly make your application stand out from the crowd. (See page 104 for more guidance on telephone calls.)

Not all companies will take telephone calls. Where you come up against this, try putting yourself in the place of the advertiser. What would you want to see in a letter? What would make you interested to meet this applicant? What skills and qualities would you be looking for?

For example, if we assume that the same job for which Ann was applying had a shorter, less detailed advertisement, it might have looked like this:

Senior Life Policy Adminstrator required. Must have three years' experience and be computer literate. Good prospects. CV to Mrs J Morgan, Personnel Manager, Ashville Assurance plc, Braintree Rd, Uxbridge, Middlesex, UB12 8OJ.

Ann would have to be creative about matching up her skills. She would have to *imagine* what was needed and list her positive qualities and experience to show that she understood what the job was *likely* to entail. Her list would be very similar to the one for the detailed advertisement, as would her letter.

You can try this too – it may take you a little longer than would a straightforward matching exercise, but it will be just as worthwhile.

Letters to advertised vacancies through agencies/consultancies

Many companies use agencies/consultancies to advertise their vacancy either on a retained basis to carry out the initial interviewing or simply to filter and pass on the responses. It should be remembered that these people may have as much power as a personnel manager in deciding who gets through to an interview. In the current economic climate, consultancies do get a much larger number of responses to their advertisements. Therefore, presenting yourself well to them is as important as it is when writing directly to a company.

Occasionally, consultancies will name their client in the advert. There really is no point in trying to bypass them by applying directly to the company – your letter and CV will simply get passed back to them. Companies have usually paid in advance to retain the consultant so they will gain nothing from seeing you directly.

One exception to this rule can be if you already have an influential contact within that organisation itself. If so, give that contact a call and say that you have seen their advert through ABC Consultancy and that you are interested in applying. This can work positively for you in two ways: (a) if the consultancy puts your CV forward, your name and your interest will be known to the company, and (b) if the contact is aware that you are on the market he or she may ask the consultancy where your CV is, and if the consultant has not seen fit to put you forward, they may question their decision. This must of course be done with great tact.

Your letter should show how you meet the client's needs, exactly as you would do when applying directly to a company. Use the matching exercise described above, but it is a good idea to end the letter on 'I will contact you in the next few days to check that my details have arrived and to discuss my application further'. You will then have the opportunity to talk them into seeing you if they have not already called you for an interview.

Example of a letter to agencies to go on to their files

Ms K Peters
Senior Consultant
Insurance Division
AJA Recruitment Ltd
185 Handley Road
Uxbridge
Middlesex
UB25 4PM

Flat 11, Highfields House
Summer Road
Enfield
Middlesex
EN4 2HG

Telephone: 0181-704 9932

4 April 1995

Dear Ms Peters,

I am interested in obtaining a new position within the Life and Pensions Administration field and your company has been recommended to me in this connection.

Please find enclosed a copy of my CV for your information, from which you will note the following:

- Three years in Pensions – two in a supervisory role, where I have carried out staff training.

- Ability to work on a variety of computerised finance systems and WP packages

- Good educational background – BTEC in Business and Finance

I would be grateful, therefore, if you would place me on your register and consider me for any current or future appointments that may be suitable, permanent or temporary. My last position became redundant following company restructure, therefore I am immediately available for work.

I will contact you within the next week to arrange a time to see you so that you may meet me to discuss my background further.

Yours sincerely,

Ann Powell
Enc.

Speculative ('cold') letters to companies

Speculative letters *do* work, even if you feel that they are a waste of time! The company may have some plans to recruit in the future, and will usually keep your details on file. Alternatively, they may have some temporary work, and a foot in the door may be all that you need to prove yourself. It may be a numbers game, but it is one with a high reward in terms of the stake.

You will not get a reply from every cold letter you send out, and please do not be too disappointed when you get negative letters back. It is just something that you need to steel yourself for – there will be lots of 'thanks but no, we'll keep you on file' type letters, but there will also be others that write back and say 'yes we might have something for you'. All you need is one of your letters to be at the right place at the right time and you may have struck gold.

You do, though, need to make it clear to the person why you are applying to that company, as opposed to any other. If you use the name of the company in the actual text of the letter itself (as in the example that follows), this has a dramatic and positive effect in response rates (in my experience 80 per cent of these cold letters get some sort of reply). The company will feel that you have made a special effort to write to them and even if they have no vacancies, will write back to you to thank you and keep you on file.

Wherever possible, you should obtain the name of the person you wish to write to if you are writing speculatively. It will at least get read by that person or their assistant, rather than being discarded at first glance.

Although you may not enjoy doing so, it is always best to follow up a speculative letter with a polite telephone call. You only need to say that you are just phoning to ask if they received your letter and if there are any opportunities that might arise in the future. It sets you aside from other applicants, and they will be more likely to remember your name and bear you in mind when they have something suitable.

Another approach on 'cold' letters is to actually use the 'negatives' to accentuate the positives. For example, if you feel that your age is likely to go against you, play on it. However, these 'negative letters' do take some practice, and should be used with caution. It is better to build up your confidence with 'normal' letters before you try this approach.

On the following pages are examples of speculative letters which cover a variety of approaches.

Product Presentation

Speculative letter to companies – example 1

Mrs T Easton
Personnel Manager
Officequip Ltd
Gardner Road
Croydon
CR3 4JY

7 Inglewood Road
Forest Hill
London
SE23 2TS

Tel. 0181-291 5534

4 February 1995

Dear Mrs Easton,

I am an experienced Engineer and have worked within a large Office Equipment company, Hartgate Distribution Ltd, for several years in a senior and supervisory role, for facsimile and photocopier machines.

I am familiar with all aspects of field service, customer liaison and organising a small team of Service Engineers, and have been thoroughly trained to a high standard in office equipment maintenance and customer care.

Officequip Ltd has established itself as a solid name in the field of information technology, an industry in which I am most interested as it is undergoing some exciting changes and a period of growth. I feel that my skills could prove useful should a position arise where you are seeking someone with my type of experience and knowledge in engineering.

I am enclosing my Curriculum Vitae for your consideration, and will, if I may, contact you within the next week or so regarding any possible temporary or permanent vacancies which may arise within Officequip, either now or in the near future.

Your sincerely,

Ben Stevens
Enc.

The Job Search Manual

Speculative letter to companies – example 2
'Eliminating the Negative' – to be used with caution!

Mr J Franks
Operations Manager
Officequip Ltd
Gardner Road
Croydon
CR3 4JY

7 Inglewood Road
Forest Hill
London
SE23 2TS

Tel: 0181-291 5534

4 February 1995

Dear Mr Franks,

No doubt you are accustomed to receiving speculative letters and CVs from a number of people. I am one of those people, and I would be most grateful if you would allow me to explain my reasons for writing to Officequip.

Firstly, I would like to say that I am 50 – and I have no experience of the IT industry. However, I do have over 20 years' experience of electrical equipment engineering and service. From my CV, you will see that I have successfully transferred from the telecommunications industry to fax and copiers and feel confident that my skills could be used by your company in the same way.

I am aware that Officequip have a growing Field Service function, which has been positively received by dealers and customers alike. Should you be in a position where you are looking for someone to enhance the department, either now or in the future, I can offer you my experience and mature approach, plus reliability, diplomacy, enthusiasm and versatility.

I would welcome the opportunity to discuss how I could make such a contribution to your company. I will, if I may, telephone you within the next week to see whether you may have a few minutes free for us to meet at a convenient time.

Yours sincerely,

Ben Stevens
Enc.

N.B. This is a genuine letter (with the details changed) that actually got one person three informal interviews!

Speculative letter to companies – example 3
Following a newspaper article that indicates company expansion/winning a new major contract, etc.

Mrs H Cotton
Personnel Manager
Good Food Restaurants Ltd
Brookbank Road
Havering
Essex
RM5 9HS

10 Walker's Way
Petts Wood
Kent
TN12 2TZ

Tel: 01980-246810

2nd October 1995

Dear Mrs Cotton,

I read in this week's edition of Hotel and Caterer that Good Food Restaurants has announced plans to open a chain of quality restaurants in the Kent area.

I anticipate that as part of this exciting development, you may be considering recruiting staff with experience in accounting for the catering industry. If so, I would very much like to be considered for any vacancies which may arise for experienced financial accountants.

As you will see from my enclosed Curriculum Vitae, I have worked at Peter's Brasserie in Petts Wood as Assistant to the Company Accountant for the past five years. This has given me a valuable insight into the hospitality industry, and I feel that I have shown the ability to work well in a busy and demanding environment. I am very interested in developing my career in the catering industry and am currently studying ACCA as a part of this development.

I would welcome the opportunity to discuss how my experience at Peter's Brasserie may be useful to Good Food Restaurants and will, if I may, telephone your secretary within the next few days to see if you are planning any interviews in the near future.

Should you wish to contact me in the meantime, please do not hesitate to do so.

Yours sincerely,

John B. Coles
Enc.

Letters to contacts asking for advice

These letters are not about asking people for a job – it is simply a way of developing your network and obtaining advice about your career. You must not put pressure on people, so it is always best to be gentle.

Handwritten letters are particularly effective when you are writing to a specific person at the suggestion of someone else, and you wish to say that 'Joe Green suggested I write to you personally'. It is so much more personal. Send your letter and CV and then follow this up with a phone call a few days later – you can always suggest an informal meeting over a coffee or drink.

> 10 Walker's Way
> Petts Wood
> Kent
> TN12 2TZ
> Tel. 01980-246810
>
> Mr H Ashton
> Finance Director
> Greens Stationery Ltd
> 33 Frederick Lane
> Bromley
> Kent
> BR5 3RG
>
> 4 October 1994
>
> Dear Mr Ashton,
>
> I was discussing career moves with Joe Green last week when he suggested that you may be able to give me some guidance on how best to proceed. I am currently working at Peter's Brasserie in Petts Wood as Assistant to the Company Accountant and am studying Stage 2 ACCA. I wish to progress my career but am undecided as to the exact direction I should take.
>
> I have enclosed my Curriculum Vitae to give you some idea on my background and as Joe tells me that you have several years' experience in financial management, I was wondering of you could spare me half an hour, possibly over a lunch time, to discuss the best way forward at my stage.
>
> If I may, I will telephone you next week to see if you have any free time. Your help would be much appreciated.
>
> Yours sincerely,
>
> John B. Coles
>
> Enc.

Application Forms

Many companies and agencies use standard application forms as a way of selecting people for interview. It enables them to get the information they require, rather than what you want to give them, and makes selecting and comparing applicants much easier. Many private and public sector employers, particularly those with Equal Opportunities Policies, use application forms as their preferred way of screening.

Although the information requested can vary widely, the same rules apply as with as CV and letter writing: the application form should get the reader interested enough in you to want to meet you or recommend you for interview so that you can have the opportunity to sell yourself to them face to face.

Many application forms ask what seem like irrelevant or difficult questions – the one that people dread most of all is where they leave a blank space asking 'why are you applying for this job?' or 'what you feel you have to offer this company?' The blank space is actually an ideal opportunity for you to tell them that you can do the job and learn new methods, even if you do not have exactly the right qualifications or experience. If you go through the matching exercise thoroughly, you should really have a good idea of the answers to these types of questions. If you are not sure why you are applying to them or what you have to offer, are you sure you are applying for the right job?

There is no way you can avoid answering direct questions about salary, but you can be approximate (so that you do not put them off by quoting too little and lose out or too much and be rejected immediately). For example, 'what salary are you looking for?' could be answered as 'c. £10-13,000'.

The golden rules of CV writing apply, and in addition it is worth remembering the following:

- Before filling in the form, either do a photocopy and fill that in first as a trial run before writing on the form itself, or write first in pencil and go over it in ink or ballpoint when you have checked it through. You only have one chance with an application form!

- The information should be the same as that on your CV as you might be asked for both.

- Avoid using jargon – the person first reading your form may not be a specialist in your field and may not understand, so you could lose out.

- Always keep a copy or at least a record of what you wrote in the form. When you attend an interview, they will use the form as a point of reference.

Telephone Applications

Whether you are applying to an advertised vacancy or approaching someone on a speculative basis, the golden rules of applying by telephone are the same as for letters.

Advertised vacancies

If an advertised vacancy provides a telephone number, you can gain the advantage by applying immediately. Your aim is to introduce yourself professionally, get an application form or prime them to receive your CV, and, only very occasionally (depending on the situation), to obtain an interview there and then.

- Go through the vacancy specification as you would when matching your skills in a letter of application. Have your ideas clear in your own mind before you telephone.

- Be professional – 'It's about this job you're advertising' does nothing for you! Have the advertisement in front of you and quote the reference number/job title. State who you are and why you are phoning.

- Do not leave messages asking someone to call you back – they rarely do and you may be seen as a nuisance if you then keep ringing when they have not returned your call.

- If there is no name given in the advertisement, when you call make a note of the name of the person you speak to so you can write to them or quote their name.

- Have enough money or phone cards with you if you are using a public telephone so that you are not interrupted by pips or cut off. Try to find a phone in a quiet area. Have a pen and paper ready to make notes or take an address, interview arrangements, travel information, etc., if you are offered an interview on the spot.

- Have a brief checklist with any questions you may want to ask about the job over the telephone to show interest and prepare you better for an interview. If you do obtain an interview, write a brief letter confirming the arrangements made (if the interview is on another day). It looks professional and shows that you are keen.

- If you are really interested in the job, ask if you can fax your CV immediately – you will gain the advantage by being first. You should be able to find a photocopying/printing type shop which will have a fax service (if not, perhaps a friend's office).

Speculative applications

Most of the above will apply, the difference being that you have no vacancy to match your skills to. However, if you have done your research thoroughly, there will be good reasons why you are approaching that company. Your attitude should have the same positive 'I could benefit your company' approach, rather than asking for any old job. If a contact of yours has suggested you speak to a particular person, ask them if you can use their name when you do make an approach. It will warm up the person on the other end of the line and increase their level of interest.

Speculative applications need not only be about asking someone for a job – refer to the section on 'Networking' (page 67).

7. Interviews

So you have succeeded in obtaining an interview. Well done! This is where all the job search skills you have learned so far can be brought together. As there are so many types of interview this section deals with the more formal ones. A network meeting is in effect an interview but you are of course just seeking information and building up your contacts. Hence you will be able to use some of the following tips in your network meetings too.

Just as you have prepared yourself thoroughly for your job search, the same level of preparation should go into your interview. It may be a cliché, but 'You only have one chance to make a first impression'! Most people dread interviews but that is usually because they simply do not know what to expect.

Being prepared helps to give you much more confidence – the more you know about the company, the job and what type of questions are likely to be asked, the less nervous you are likely to be. Do remember that you are there to assess them as much as they are assessing you.

Not all interviews will be carried out by experienced or trained people, particularly in a small company or even a large one where you are meeting a junior manager. Some interviews are formal, others may be just a chat in the pub! Whatever the situation, treat each one seriously – this could be chance for a superb career move.

The Interviewer's Role

Although an interview is not really a conversation between equals (as the interviewer is in a position of greater power), it is worth remembering that they have a problem – they have a need for someone to do a job and they are hoping that the next person who walks in through the door will be the solution. They are often just busy people who would like to fill the job as quickly as possible and get back to their other work. As just mentioned, not all interviewers are experienced and they may be nervous too.

Interviewers rarely set out to be nasty for the sake of it or to trick you; they are simply doing their best to find out all they can about you and your suitability for the job. If that means they have to ask some pointed questions, they will do so to reassure themselves that they are making the right choice. We all know of horror stories where someone had an awful interview with a really tough person, but these are the exception – honestly! Interviewers do have a responsibility towards the company and the other staff to ensure that anyone they choose is the best match; they often have to justify their choice or even answer to someone else if their decision proves to be a poor one.

Your Role

Your prime aim as an interviewee, therefore, is to remove any doubts that the interviewer may have about your suitability for the job. One of the best ways for you to achieve this is to prepare yourself thoroughly in advance. After all, actors research their roles and rehearse to ensure that they give the best performance. The interview is no different.

If you can run through an interview with a friend before you go for the real thing, it really does help. Of course, you do not know exactly what will be asked and what the interviewer will be like, but there are some pretty standard questions that come up again and again.

It is worth remembering that the interviewer has probably selected your CV from one of many, and will therefore have an expectation that you can do the job (or a good deal of it).

An experienced interviewer will have prepared something along the following lines (the example shown here is called the 'Seven Point Plan'):

Job description:

- Title
- Job purpose
- Location
- Position in organisation/authority
- Main contacts of the job
- Objectives of the role
- Responsibilities/activities and duties

Employee specification (some of these things may be more or less important than others – for example, physique and strength would be important for a warehouseman but not for an office worker):

(1) Physical
    Physique   height, strength, hearing, sight
    Appearance   looks, grooming, standard of dress
    Health / voice / age

(2) Attainments
    Education   level, subjects and grades
    Experience   nature, duration, knowledge, skills
    Job training

(3) General intelligence   possibly using tests or types of questions

(4) Special aptitudes   mechanical / verbal / numerical / artistic

(5) Interests   intellectual / practical / social / physical / artistic

(6) Disposition (i.e. personality)
    Acceptability in general terms
    Solitary / outgoing
    Leader / follower
    Suitability for this company / job
    Attitude to authority, responsibility and change
    Future career goals

(7) Circumstances
    Age
    Dependants / wife / husband
    Housing
    Mobility / driver

EARLY PREPARATION

Matching your skills to the job specification

Find out about the job, what experience and skills are required and what the responsibilities will be. Get a full job specification, if you can.

Write down a list of the things that you feel make you suitable for the job; use the matching method again. Do the same with things that may cause doubts about you, e.g. any gaps in your career, any jobs you were sacked from, any lack of experience in areas where they want a particular type, etc. This will help you to prepare yourself for any difficult questions and have suitable answers ready (without learning them parrot-fashion).

Company information

Find out as much as you can about the company. The more information you have, the better. If you show that you are well-informed and intelligent, it will help to shift the 'power balance' between you and the interviewer – they will find it much harder to play superior.

Place and journey

Make sure that you have the full address, which division you should report to, that you know how to get there and how long the journey will take (remember to take the rush hour into account). If you will be driving, find out where you can park. It may be worthwhile to do a trial run beforehand so that you will know all these points.

Your questions

Prepare a neatly written or typed list of questions that you may want to ask (but not about money, holidays or benefits – see below).

Decide what you're going to wear

Try on your outfit (see below) and make sure that it is clean and pressed. If you are wearing new shoes to the interview break them in a couple of days before – you may be very glad you did!

Salary

You may be able to find out in advance about the salary on offer. When you are going through an agency, or have responded to an advertisement, the salary range is often given. If not, then you can safely assume that the interviewer will have read your CV and will have a vague idea of what you earn (even if you did not put it on your CV). You would not usually have been invited for interview if they thought that you were either way above or way below what they are paying.

ON THE DAY

Dress and presentation

Appearances are extremely important; research has shown that people form around 80 per cent of their opinion of you very early in the interview. Never dress casually (unless you are going for a job where a smart outfit really would be out of place such as building or decorating – though you must still be clean and look as if you have made an effort). If you look good on the outside, you will feel good on the inside.

Men should stick to dark colours (a suit is really a must), black socks, and go easy on the after-shave. If you wear an earring or have long hair, please take out the earring and tie your hair back. You may feel that they can take or leave you as you are, but if you stand out as too different, they will leave you – be assured of that! The choice is yours.

For women, avoid too much jewellery or perfume and very flashy outfits. You are going for a job and not there to be judged just on your fashion sense (unless of course you are going for a job where it is crucial such as modelling or fashion).

Paperwork

It is a good idea to clear out your briefcase or bag before you go. A cluttered one gives a disorganised impression and it can be embarrassing to fumble around looking for papers.

Take your up-to-date CV with you even if you have already sent one – you may have to fill in an application form when you arrive, and you will be able to transfer the information easily and accurately from your CV. Take paper and a pen so that you can make notes at the interview if you need to.

On arrival at the company

Be on time, preferably five to ten minutes early to use the washroom and gather your thoughts before you go in. If you feel your heart racing, go to the washroom and sigh out sharply a few times – this will help to calm you and release tension.

If you are going to be late, always telephone and ask to speak to the interviewer or their assistant. Avoid leaving a message with anyone else if possible, as it may not get through to the right person. If you do arrive late, apologise sincerely but briefly. Long rambling excuses can sound unconvincing.

Be polite to everyone you meet, whoever they are; they may be asked their opinion of you later. The tea lady may have been there for years and may be friendly with the MD! Never assume that all females are secretarial staff – the receptionist may be someone senior sitting in during a lunch break, for example. Be friendly and cheerful and thank them personally if they have made you coffee.

Never smoke while you are waiting; you will smell unpleasant, especially if the interviewer is a non-smoker. If you have a really dry mouth, ask for a glass of water while you are waiting. Alternatively, imagine sucking a piece of sharp lemon – your mouth will start to water.

THE INTERVIEW ITSELF

Nervousness

Nervousness is normal and can help to gear you up nicely. However, if you are extremely nervous it will make you and the interviewer feel embarrassed. Remember that they are human too (usually!) and they want to fill the job as much as you might want it to be offered to you.

Greeting and handshake

Smile and be friendly with the interviewer, and use their surname until told otherwise. Shake hands firmly if they offer theirs. Try not to crush them or, worse, to give them a limp, weak handshake; they will get the impression that you are a weak person. Always thank them for seeing you when you greet them. Many interviewers start off with small talk to relax you but this may not mean that the rest of the interview will be informal.

Body language

Body language is vitally important – it is one of the things that can instantly make people get on well or badly. Your body language should convey enthusiasm and confidence.

Wait until you are invited to sit down and, depending on the seating arrangements, try to 'match' their body language – if they lean forward slightly do the same. But if they lean right away from you, you will make them uncomfortable if you try to get even closer. Never ever lounge back too far yourself – it can appear 'laid back' or even arrogant, as can putting your arms around the back of your head when you are getting into conversation.

Eye contact is important; look at them when you or they speak, but do not stare. Nervousness can make you do this, so be aware. If you find eye contact difficult, look at the bridge of their nose – they will think you are looking them in the eye.

Do watch for signs that the interviewer is losing interest – fidgeting, tapping their pen, flicking through their notes, etc. If you see this happening you may be rambling off on a tangent. Be aware too that your facial expressions can give you away: a sarcastic smile when you are asked about your last job or boss can do a lot of damage to the interviewer's opinion of you!

Communication

Communication is not just about talking, it is about listening too. Listen carefully to the interviewer, show that you are interested and nod from time to time. Communication is a 'loop' between people and should be an exchange of information.

Always answer the question they have asked; try not to ramble on or go off on a tangent and keep your answers concise and punchy without giving 'yes and no' answers. Listen hard to the question – if you do not understand it, ask them if they would mind clarifying that point. Avoid firing off answers without first pausing for a second – it gives you time to think about what they are really asking and to give a relevant answer.

You do not have to get into a 'they ask, you answer, they ask, you answer' situation; you too can ask questions as you go along. Try to make it as normal a conversation as possible. It is a two-way street and also a chance for you to show that you have done your research and preparation.

Matching yourself to the job

Match yourself to the job and the company whenever the opportunity arises, by using comparisons with previous experiences, and by suggesting that your knowledge in that particular area could be useful to them.

One powerful way of getting people to feel that you are just the person for the job is to use the word 'we' – e.g. if you are asked how you would do a particular thing, show that you are automatically assuming that you are a part of the company by saying, 'We could do this, or we could do that'.

Be yourself

You are perfectly entitled to have opinions, so do not be afraid to voice them (tactfully) as long as they are not likely to offend anyone. But leave the soap box at home! Never interrupt or argue with the interviewer even if you disagree – it will get you both annoyed and you will certainly come across as a potential trouble-maker.

Try not to be too familiar. This can make the interviewer feel uncomfortable or threatened. This sometimes happens when you are nervous and the interviewer is friendly – be careful you do not respond by being over-friendly.

Never swear, use slang or tell lots of jokes. A sense of humour is one thing, but employers are looking for a serious attitude to work.

Don't smoke

They might be anti-smokers. If they are smoking and invite you to do so, on the whole it is best to say 'no thank you' anyway; you may have to meet someone else at the company who is a non-smoker.

Tell the truth

If you lie, it will probably show and they will usually be able to find out anyway. Of course, if, for example, you did not get on with your boss, you need not be too painfully honest – use your judgement.

Sell your strengths

There is no need to draw attention to your weaknesses. If they do, you will already have worked out your answers in advance. Show that you are confident, but not too much or they may worry that you might annoy potential colleagues.

Never criticise

It is just not done to be rude or critical about your past employers or companies, no matter how negative you may feel. Be positive at all times; they are not looking for a bitter, negative or depressed person – would you?

Don't name-drop or bring out references

People hate name-droppers! Keep references, letters or samples of your work to yourself unless you are asked. Paperwork usually detracts from the personal nature of the interview and you are there because you can do the job – you should not need 'props'.

Salary

Always wait for the interviewer to bring up the question of salary and when they do, you can ask them (without being pushy) what range they have in mind. This will give you an idea while showing the interviewer that you are not concerned with the details at this stage.

When you are asked what salary you are looking for, it is wise to give a general answer – one that indicates that although the money is, of course, important, you are keen to find out about the job itself as it may have different responsibilities than your last job. If you are specific too early on, you may be ruled out before you have really had the chance to sell yourself. Once you have and the company wants you, you will be in a much stronger position to negotiate.

Thank the interviewer

Remember to thank them for their time when you leave. It is fine to ask when you may expect a decision – again it shows that you are keen.

OTHER TYPES OF INTERVIEW

Panel interviews

Some organisations will use panel interviews (where more than one person is seeing you at the same time). There are several advantages to using such a process:

- It allows several people with whom you would potentially be working to meet you and see if you would fit into the team.

- It ensures fairer selection than that of allowing just one person's view (or 'gut feeling') to work in favour or against you.

- It saves time – interviewing in 'one fell swoop' rather than several interviews with different people.

- It shows how you interact with a group and cope with the pressure of several people asking questions of you.

There is no typical interview panel but generally speaking it will comprise people who have a direct interest in the role, which would usually include a manager or two, a supervisor and a personnel representative.

The preparation which you should carry out for a panel interview is exactly the same as for a one-to-one. In addition, though, if you can find out who is going to be on the panel, what their interest is in this position, plus any information about their own job, you will feel much more confident about the interview. Once you have entered the interview room, try and bear these golden rules in mind:

- Greet *everyone* as they introduce themselves – do not ignore the secretary taking notes if one is present. Try to remember their names and role as they are introduced.

- When you are asked a question by one of the panel, address your answer directly to him or her but do look round at the other interviewers as you answer.

- If you are fired a series of questions from more than one person, do not panic! Smile and say something like 'These are all interesting questions, but may I take one at a time?' Go to the first questioner and say 'You asked me about .....?' and answer the question. Then do the same with the others. This will show that you can remain calm on the firing line and that you can take each question logically.

- If you find one interviewer repeatedly asking difficult questions (or even showing an obvious dislike towards you) do bring the rest of the group into your eye contact when you answer. This will help to bolster your confidence – there is usually at least one person who will be friendly towards you. Whatever you do though, do not ignore the difficult person – he or she may put you down to the rest of the group when they discuss the interview later.

- When you ask questions, address them to the person who is likely to be most interested in that particular matter. For example, you could ask the personnel manager about how they appraise performance and ask the department supervisor about their computer systems.

- When the interview is coming to a close, thank them all for their time.

Sequential interviews

These are usually one-to-one interviews but with several people on the same day. The reasons for using this method are not unlike that of a panel interview, apart from the group element. Each interviewer may have a free range as to what they would like to ask you, or may have specific questions that will not be covered by anyone else.

In all cases, when you are asked a question that you answered only half an hour before with another interviewer, do answer the question with the same sincerity as if you were doing so for the first time. When you are asked if you have any questions, and you feel that you have run out of things to ask, you can at least say that you asked Mr A about so and so, and would the interviewer like to add anything to that?

Assessment centres

These are becoming more popular as they enable several people to be interviewed at one time, and will usually consist of some or all of the following:

- A one-to-one interview
- A problem-solving exercise – either alone or in the group

- A group activity of some kind
- A written exercise
- A role play
- A psychometric test

Generally speaking, the assessment is usually designed around what are known as 'key competencies' – that is, the skills, attributes, experience and personal qualities that are needed to do the job. The exercises aim to give concrete evidence as to whether or not you have these competencies. This makes the selection process much fairer.

The one-to-one interview aspect will be the same as previously outlined, but there are some special considerations for the group activities where several of you are candidates, either for the same job or different jobs in the organisation. When you are asked to carry out a group exercise, it can be hard to know what the employer really wants from you. There will usually be people observing the group, which can be a little nerve-wracking! For instance, should you be the leader or should you follow someone else in the group? Should you argue your point or agree with the others? In my view it is simply best to be yourself. Would you want to take a job where you had to be the leader if that is not your character (or vice versa)? If you assume a personality different from your own the observer may sense that something is wrong.

The golden rule is to listen to other people's points of view but make sure that yours is heard – without being aggressive. Do not try to win by showing off or putting someone else down. Beware also of sitting back and letting the others do all the work; make every effort to be involved whilst involving the others in the group.

Psychometric assessment

Aptitude tests and personality questionnaires are forms of psychometric assessment used by some employers as part of the selection process. They are used primarily because they can often provide more objective, reliable (and therefore fairer) information about a candidate than the more subjective assessment of a personal interview where sometimes 'gut feelings' can take over. Some employers will ask applicants to take an initial test before they decide on whether or not to invite you for interview. Others will use tests with the results considered as just one part of the selection procedure.

Aptitude tests

Aptitude tests measure your ability to reason, interpret and analyse. They are administered under strict test conditions – it is rare to finish all the tasks within the time limit. The results are used to help predict how successful you will be in your chosen career.

Some commonly used tests evaluate your ability to:

- Recognise relationships between words
- Evaluate the logic of given statements
- Recognise relationships between numbers
- Interpret data from statistical tables
- Follow diagrammatically coded instructions
- Recognise diagrammatic relationships
- Manipulate three-dimensional shapes into two dimensions

You are unlikely to be asked to do them all. While verbal and numerical reasoning tests are used for many types of work, diagrammatic reasoning tests are often used for computer programming and spatial reasoning tests for work which requires good spatial awareness (e.g. design, technology).

You can prepare for aptitude tests in several ways. For youngsters, in most careers services you can sit a test battery which is then scored so that you see how well you did in relation to others who have taken the test. You may also be able to sit a separate numeracy test. Some tests do not allow you to use a calculator so brush up on your mental arithmetic! You could also practise by doing word games, mathematical teasers, puzzles with diagrams and so forth. Or you could read Eysenck's *Know your own IQ*, or Barrett and Williams' *Test your Own Aptitude* (both available in paperback). *How to Master Selection Tests*, published by Kogan Page, is very useful.

Personality questionnaires

Personality questionnaires are used to find out about you as an individual. They are usually untimed and there are no right or wrong answers. It is in your own interests to answer the questions as honestly as possible since the results will be used to judge whether you are personally suited to the type of work you are seeking and whether you will fit in with the working environment and demands of the job. Preparation is neither appropriate nor possible! Just answer the questions as honestly as you can. Don't agonise over your responses – there are no rights or wrongs.

Interviews

Examples of Interview Questions

If you look back at your self-assessment questions you will be surprised at how many of those questions will actually be asked about you by the interviewer. They want to find out your strengths and weaknesses and your skills and potential in the same way that you did. The following examples are presented in a random order.

- **Tell me about your last job.**
  Give a description of what the job involved, with particular emphasis on: the duties that are similar to the job here, the way in which you helped the company, the skills which you used and your responsibilities, your career progression if you were promoted and so forth.

- **What parts of the job did you really enjoy?**
  Make these relevant to the job for which you are applying and match the two together.

- **Why did you leave / are you leaving the company?**
  Whatever your reason for leaving, always be positive. Saying that you did not get on with the boss is hardly encouraging for the interviewer! If you left due to ill health but you are fit now, stress this. If you left work to have a family, and you did something that 'kept your hand in', mention that too. If the job was made redundant say so without making it personal or sounding bitter – 'it was just one of those things'.

- **What do you think of the company now?**
  Again, avoid being negative in any way and please do not whinge! A potential employer wants to feel that you are a loyal person with a positive attitude. No matter what the circumstances for you leaving or wishing to leave your company, talk in glowing terms about, for example, the products, the people, the quality of service.

- **Tell me about yourself.**
  A lot of people dread this question but it really is one that you can prepare in advance, and gives you a superb opportunity to give them all your positive qualities/experience in one go. The question is not asking you to give a life history, but a brief snapshot of you and your work. It is important to talk about your personal life but not into too much detail – a simple sentence or two should be enough. Then give a brief 'rundown' of your career to date, mentioning your achievements, finishing off with your current situation.

- **What are your ambitions / career plans?**
  Never be too specific: if you say you want promotion soon then they will be suspicious that you may not last in this job for long. Neither should you talk about a particular position that you would like to reach – the same applies. Be general, saying that you are ambitious in that you want to do well and be recognised for your efforts, and are keen to develop your skills further. Smart answers such as 'I want your job' are simply not smart.

- **Have you got experience of...?**
  Always try to find something similar to the question and prove that you have by describing an actual experience. Bring in the job specification by saying that was one of the things that attracted you to the job. If you do not have the right experience or anything close to it, emphasise your keenness to learn and give an example of something that you learned quickly in the past – for example, any training you have had, relevant hobbies and interests, someone you know who has done the job and how much you have found out about it, your personal qualities that show you can do that part of the job.

- **Why do you want to work for this company?**
  A chance for you to show that you have taken the trouble to find out about them. You can talk about their products, their reputation as a growing company, the type of work they do, the fact that you can contribute a great deal to them because of your knowledge and skills.

- **Why have you applied for this particular job?**
  The answer should be similar to the one above. List your skills/qualities/experience and match them to the job – for example, 'I've done x and y for the past six months so I feel that I would very quickly learn how this company does a and b. The job looks interesting and there seems plenty of scope for me to develop.'

- **How do you feel about working for a competitor to your last company?**
  This one is often asked when you are applying to a similar company. You need to stress that you have no doubts that you can contribute as much to this company as to the last one, and the fact that they are competitors really is not important.

- **We can't match your last salary – what are you looking for?**
  See Chapter 8 on negotiating salary.

- **What did you most dislike about your last job?**
  There is no need to be too honest about hating paperwork! There are always aspects in any job that you like more or less than others, but it is important not to make these a big issue. It is better to say that most of the work was enjoyable and although sometimes the routine tasks were less enjoyable, they did not bother you and you always got them done.

- **What do you feel were your major achievements whilst you were there?**
  You should know these well by now. Remember that even though you may think your job gave little scope for achievements, there is always something you can use – for example, setting up a new filing system, working well with the team, finishing a particular project on time, and so forth.

- **How would your colleagues describe you?**
  This can be difficult if you are not comfortable with boasting. But if you say that you hope they would consider you were hardworking, sociable, a team player, good at your job, took your job seriously, for example, this does not sound too over the top. Be positive. Blow your own trumpet because no one else will do it for you!

- **Do you prefer working in a team or on your own?**
  Avoid being too specific – the job may require both. It is advisable to say that as long as the job keeps you busy and interested, you are happy with a mixture of team work and being left to use your own initiative. You will still get things done.

- **What motivates you?**
  Never say 'money' unless you are going for a top-flight sales job! Doing a good job, feeling satisfied with what you and the department are achieving, working well with a good company, are all strong answers.

- **What are your strengths?**
  Give a list of your positive qualities – by now you should be clear in your own mind. If you have done your matching exercise before you get to the interview, then you should be able to make them specific to the job.

- **What about your weaknesses?**
  Do not give them any real weaknesses if you can help it! If the mood is right you can use humour – for example, 'Chocolate!' If you are pushed, give them a weakness that is not crucial to doing the job well. Do not

make it personal about your character, the way you get on with other people or your lack of experience for this particular job. You could say something like, 'Well, no one's perfect but I don't think that I have any weaknesses that would affect my ability to do a good job for you'.

- **What do you think makes a good manager?**
  This is asked either when you are going for a management job or when someone is trying to assess how you respond to authority. General qualities such as fairness, the ability to delegate, encourage and support staff, take responsibility, see the big picture, set targets and deliver results, are good answers.

- **Why should we give you this job rather than anyone else?**
  There is no way you can compare yourself against the competition – you do not know who or what they are. For example, 'I don't know who I'm competing against for this job so I can't comment on their suitability, but I do know that I'm hardworking, have the right experience and skills for this job and I feel that I would fit in very well here.'

- **Have you made any other job applications?**
  Do not be too precise here. If you have been making other applications you must stress that this job is the one where you are particularly keen as it seems such a good fit. Even if this job is not your top favourite among others you have applied for, do not let it show! You must not put them off in any way – give yourself the opportunity to choose when you have more than one offer.

- **Do you have any questions?**
  When all your questions have been asked during the course of the interview, it is perfectly acceptable to say so as long as you have found out all you need to know about the job and what would be expected of you. This would usually be the case where the interview has been a two-way conversation. In a way, it compliments the interviewer on a good interview.

  But if you have not asked any questions before, you really should do so now. You need to leave the interviewer with a lasting impression – your questions can be crucial here. Therefore, it is always advisable to draw up a list of questions in advance about the company and the position – but not about money, perks or holidays. You need to convince them that you are genuinely interested in the job rather than how much it will pay you.

  You can also use your questions to highlight any particular skills you have that would benefit the company; this can be useful where the interviewer has not covered a particular area where you feel you really have something extra to offer. Here are some examples of questions which would apply to most jobs:

- Of all the responsibilities of this job, what do you think are the most important?
- Can you tell me a little about the rest of the team in the department?
- Who would I be working with for most of the time?
- What would I be doing in the first week if I am offered the job?
- Does the company have a written policy on customer service?
- What type of management style does the company have?
- What computer systems do you use here?
- Would my experience of helping junior staff to learn be useful here?
- Is there any training that you feel I would benefit from?
- At my last company I was also responsible for ...; would you like me to help in that area here?
- Does the company plan to extend its products or services?
- What type of preparation would you like me to do before I started the job if I am successful?
- How do you appraise staff?
- I enjoy finding new ways to improve systems and procedures. Will there be scope for me to put my ideas forward when appropriate?

After the Interview

As soon as the interview is over, go somewhere quiet and make some notes of how you think it went. Ask yourself 'What did I do well?' and 'What could I have done better?' If any really difficult questions were asked, you can learn from them and prepare yourself for the future. Try to avoid the temptation to rush and see your family or friends straightaway; you need time to think things through and assess how it went. It is difficult to do that with people around asking questions.

Make a note of any information you were given at the interview that will help you to assess if it is the type of job/company you are looking for. Think about what you would do if they ask you back for another interview or offer you the job – would you say yes? What more would you need to know about the job to make a decision? What questions would you have next time? You may be asked back for a second interview, so do keep a note of everything you learned at the first stage.

Two days after the interview, if you are interested in the vacancy and the company, write a brief letter to the interviewer. This helps to ensure that you stand out from the crowd. It is common courtesy to thank someone for their time and, in addition, it gives you the opportunity to confirm your interest and restate what you feel you have to offer.

If you have not heard from the company by the date they gave you, it is perfectly acceptable to telephone and ask them politely if they have made a decision. If you are not offered the job, although you may find this difficult, it may be a good idea to find out why. Some companies will not tell you, others may give you a good reason. Remember that you were probably not the only one going for the job and as you have no way of knowing what the competition was, there is no point in taking it too personally if you are rejected, especially if you feel that it was a good interview and you did your best.

8. THE NEGOTIATION AND SALE

The Offer

When you are offered a job, unless you are absolutely convinced that it is right in every way, do not give an immediate answer. Show that you are very pleased to have been offered, and that you would like to think about it and come back to them within a day (or two days if you prefer) with an answer. If you want more than they are offering, this will give you time to work out if there is anything you can do to increase the offer.

Be prepared to make concessions. A good career move might mean that you have to take less than you were looking for, but the long-term gains could be much greater. Also, there may be a probationary period or a set date to review your salary so do not dismiss an offer without first taking these into account. Remember that the salary may be part of a package, which can contain any of the following (depending on the seniority of the position):

Bonus
Share options
Mortgage subsidy
Interest-free season ticket loan
Pension
Relocation expenses
Sports and social facilities
Study leave
Annual (or sooner) reviews
Commission

Profit share
Life insurance
Car or car allowance
Health insurance
Paid holidays
Staff discounts
Training or training allowance
Cost of living (e.g. geographical) adjustment

More Than One Offer?

Again, consider more than just the base salary; take into account the responsibilities, the people with whom you will be working, the travelling, and all the other items in the above list. It can help to talk the offers through with your family or a friend. Drawing up a list of pros and cons for each job is also very helpful: seeing things in writing is usually easier.

Stalling on an offer if you are awaiting the outcome of another interview is never easy, but you can buy time as described above. If the job you are waiting to hear about is through an agency, tell the agency that you have had another offer but that you are very keen on their client. They may be able to get a response for you.

If the job is not through an agency, you can phone the company and politely ask when you can expect a decision. If the second offer is not forthcoming but you still prefer the first job, then you will have to make a tough decision: to risk losing the first one if you keep stalling them, or to stall them and find that the second one is not offered. Again, talk this through with your family.

Wait until you actually get an offer letter before handing in your notice (if you are working) or before accepting one job in writing if you are expecting a definite offer letter from another.

Starting Your New Job

Once you have accepted a new job there will always be a period of readjustment, so do expect some minor changes to your usual way of working. You may be on a probationary period, so it is important to maintain the momentum and enthusiasm which actually got you the job in the first place. You may find it useful to read *On the Way Up,* by Simon Carne (published by Management Books 2000).

After three months have passed, it is worth sitting down and thinking about how things are going. If there are some changes that can or need to be made (either to your own role or perhaps in your way of doing things) this can be a good time to do so. Hopefully, your new manager will have planned a review meeting so that you can discuss your progress. If, for any reason, you are having difficulties or the job has not been quite as you had hoped, you can talk this through. You may find it useful to go back to your notes at the beginning of this manual when you decided what you wanted and what you had to offer. If your skills are not being used fully, are there any ways in which you could bring these more into the job? Most employers will admire your initiative and will listen to your ideas.

One final point: always keep your CV up to date. This is will be extremely helpful to you if you are going for promotion or if you move jobs in the future. Add your new experiences, skills and achievements as they happen. You will find that it helps to keep you on track in your career planning.

> I hope that this manual has been helpful to you. It has been compiled as a result of working with many people looking for work – the challenges they have faced, the difficulties they have encountered and the successes they have enjoyed. I hope that you too will be successful.
>
> As I stated at the beginning, a successful job search requires a huge amount of effort from you. If you have worked through this manual, you will have seen just how much there is to do. I wish you the very best of luck.

INDEX

Achievements, 33
Action plan, 19, 70-1
Advertised vacancies, 91, 95-96, 104
Advertisements, 78, 88
Advice for small businesses, 74
AIDA, 32, 90
Answering machines, 18
Application forms, 103
Aptitude tests, 118
Asking for advice, 102
Assessing yourself, 6
Assessment centres, 116

Bailiffs, 29
Banks, 73
Body language, 112
Budget planner, 30
Business start-up, 74

Career change, 72
Careers centres, 72
Ceefax, 60
Chambers of Commerce, 59
Child support, 29
Citizens' Advice Bureau, 28-9
Cold letters, 98
Communication, 112
Company research, 65
Correspondence
    covering letters, 90-7
    speculative letters, 66, 98-101
Council tax, 24
Council tax benefit, 25
Covering letters, 90-7
Credit cards, 28
CV checklist, 48-57
CV content, 37
CVs, 32-57, 62

Debts, 28
Department of Social Security (DSS), 21
'Dial a Job', 64
Dress and presentation, 110
DSS leaflets, 22

Employee specification, 108
Employment agencies, 31, 61
Equal opportunities policies, 103
Executive Grapevine, 61

FIMBRA, 27
Financial advice, 26
Fuel, 28
Further education, 72

Getting organised, 18

Handwritten letters, 102
Headhunters, 62
Hire purchase, 29
Housing benefit, 24-5

IFA, 26
Income support, 24
Income tax, 26
Independent financial adviser, 26
Inspector of taxes, 26
Insurances, 27
Interview questions, 119-23
Interview
    paperwork, 110
Interviewer's role, 106
Interviews, 106
    dress, 110
Invalidity benefits, 25

Job centres, 63
Job clubs, 64

Job description, 107
Job fairs, 64
Job offer, 125
Job papers, 60

Law society, 74
Lawyers for enterprise, 74
Legal action, 4
Libraries, 59
Loans, 28
Local newspapers, 59-60

Maintenance, 29
Market surveys, 76
Matching yourself to the job, 113
Moneylenders, 29
Mortgages, 27

National Association for Education and Guidance Services for Adults, 72
National insurance, 22, 26
National newspapers, 59
Negative letters, 100
Nervousness, 111
Networking, 66-7, 82
New client advisers, 22
Newspapers, 59-60
    local, 59
    national, 59
    trade, 59
NI records, 26

Open university, 72
Oracle, 60

Panel interviews, 115
Paperwork, 110
Part-time employment, 73
Pensions, 27
Personal qualities, 11
Personality questionnaires, 118
Professional institutions, 63
Profile, 57
Psychometric assessment, 117

Radio advertisements, 60
Record keeping, 19
Recruitment agencies, 86
Recruitment consultancies, 61
Redundancy, 4
Reference books. 75-7
Register agencies, 61
Rent, 27

Research, 58
Resumés, 57
Retraining, 72

Salary, 110, 114, 125
Salary rates, 31
Sample CVs, 40-7
Search consultancies, 62
Selection consultancies, 62
Self-employment, 73
Sequential interviews, 116
Seven point plan, 107
Sickness benefits, 25
Social fund, 24
Social security freeline service, 22
Speculative applications, 105
Speculative letters, 66, 84, 98-101
Starting a new job, 126
State benefits, 21
Stationery, 19
Studying, 72

Target setting, 20
TECs, 74
Telephone applications, 104
Telephones, 18
Teletext, 60
Television, 60
Temporary work, 73
Trade associations, 63, 73
Trade fairs, 63
Trade newspapers, 59
Trade press, 60
Training and enterprise councils, 73-4
Training companies, 72

Unemployment benefit, 23
Unemployment Benefit Office, 22
Unemployment
    attitude, 1
    disaster or opportunity?, 1
    keeping perspective, 2
    prejudices, 3

Vacancies, 58-71, 78-9
    networking, 66
    research, 58
    sources, 58-7

ALSO AVAILABLE FROM MANAGEMENT BOOKS 2000

Super Job Search
The Complete Manual for Job-Seekers and Career-Changers
Peter K Studner

(PB, £12.99, 352pp, 246mm x 189mm, ISBN: 1-85252-030-2)

For the first time, here is a manual that has helped thousands of men and women learn the secrets behind a successful career change. Whether you are about to make your first job search or are in mid-career or even seeking to re-enter the job market, *Super Job Search* will guide you through each step of the way to land the best of possible jobs.

Written by a master career counsellor, former chief executive and board member of a number of companies in the UK, France and the US. Peter K Studner is an outplacement consultant's consultant. He has helped thousands of people with their career transitions and trains other career professionals to deliver this easy-to-follow programme. This UK edition has been specially adapted by Professor Malcolm McDonald of the Cranfield School of Management.

'**We have counselled over 2,000 individuals each one of whom we have provided with a copy of *Super Job Search*... Without question the most definitive book ever written on the subject.**' Ray Howell, Managing Director, Bridford Career Management Ltd

'**One of the most exhaustive guides on how to find a job...**' Korn/Ferry (world's largest executive recruitment agency)

'**This book makes finding the right job a proper marketing exercise just as filling the right job has become one for an employer. Both start with a rigorous review of who you are and what you can become.**' Simon H. Barrow, Chief Executive, Charles Barker Human Resources

'*Super Job Search* **turned my life around. I can't recommend this book enough to anyone wishing to succeed in a job change...**' G. D. (candidate)

Available from leading booksellers.
To order by phone on a 7-day trial, ring 01235-815544 now (credit cards accepted – full refund if returned in 7 days)

ALSO AVAILABLE FROM MANAGEMENT BOOKS 2000

Build Your Own Rainbow
A Workbook for Career and Life Management
Barrie Hopson and Mike Scally

(PB, £15.00, 192pp, 290 x 200mm, ISBN: 1-85252-074-4)

This book consists of a number of exercises designed to help you to analyse and develop your personal skills, aptitudes and ambitions. It provides the key to a number of essential career development skills, including:

- Knowing Yourself
- Learning from Experience
- Research Skills
- Setting Objectives and Making Action Plans
- Making Decisions
- Looking after Yourself
- Communicating

In carrying out the exercises in this book you will discover what is important to you about your work, your interests, your transferable skills, your most comfortable career pattern. You will be helped to set personal and career objectives and make action plans to take greater charge of yourself and your life.

Using a new system for classifying jobs and courses devised specifically for this book, your own personal profile can be checked against jobs, education and training opportunities and leisure pursuits to help widen your range of possibilities.

For 16 years, Barrie Hopson and Mike Scally of Lifeskills Management Group have run workshops on career and life management all over the world, in companies, universities, colleges, health and social care systems. Their programme has now been produced in this do-it-yourself workbook for adults who wish to make their lives more as they would like them to be.

Available from leading booksellers.
To order by phone on a 7-day trial, ring 01235-815544 now (credit cards accepted – full refund if returned in 7 days)

> ALSO AVAILABLE FROM MANAGEMENT BOOKS 2000

Changing Course
A Positive Approach to a New Job or Lifestyle
Maggie Smith

(PB, £15.00, 176pp, 290mm x 200mm, ISBN: 1-85252-161-9)

If you are – or think you are – approaching a 'mid-life crisis' and feel uncertain, dissatisfied or disappointed about your career, or life in general, this is the book for you. Major life change can be stressful but it can also be a positive and highly motivational part of our lives. The theme of this well designed workbook is the management of change and how it affects your life and the lives of those who will be affected by your decisions. *Changing Course* includes 24 exercises and explores such areas as:

- What is work?
- Money – how much is enough?
- Managing change
- Time management
- Job searching
- Self-employment
- Physical, mental and spiritual health
- Stress management

Changing Course is essential reading for anyone considering mid-life change and is also relevant for organisations interested in providing early retirement.

ABOUT THE AUTHOR

Maggie Smith is Director of Branching Out, a consultancy based in West Yorkshire specialising in the management of change for individuals and organisations. She designs programmes in Career Transitions, Counselling Skills, Stress Management and Mid-life Planning.

Available from leading booksellers.
To order by phone on a 7-day trial, ring 01235-815544 now (credit cards accepted – full refund if returned in 7 days)

> ALSO AVAILABLE FROM MANAGEMENT BOOKS 2000

Face Your Next Interview with Confidence

Jack Gratus

(PB, £9.99, 184pp, 216 x 135mm, ISBN: 1-85252-163-5)

Do you shudder at the thought of going to interviews? Do they seem to last for ever? Do you leave thinking, 'What a mess I made of that!'? Would you like to be able to project yourself as a confident, effective interviewee?

Jack Gratus has been dubbed by the media 'the King of Interviews'. This book sets out his well-known PQRSTU system for the winning interview. It shows how to:

- overcome pre-interview nerves
- get yourself into a positive mood
- listen creatively
- answer questions convincingly
- establish a good relationship with your interviewer
- handle stress interviews
- make a compelling case
- end the interview in your favour
- evaluate your performance

Jack Gratus has been conducting seminars and classes in interviewing for the last 15 years. He wrote and presented two series on interviewing for BBC television and has written and produced a number of books and training videos on the subject.

'**Essential reading. Packed with sound advice on preparing, getting through and following up interviews.**' *Nine to Five*

'**Will help you understand how interviews operate and turn them to your advantage.**' *First Voice*

> *Available from leading booksellers.*
> *To order by phone on a 7-day trial, ring 01235-815544 now (credit cards accepted – full refund if returned in 7 days)*